Visual
Computing

VISUAL COMPUTING

Richard Mark Friedhoff
Mark S. Peercy

Scientific American Library
A division of HPHLP
New York

Text Design: Cambraia (Magalhaes) Fernandes

Library of Congress Cataloging-in-Publication Data

Friedhoff, Richard Mark.
    Visual computing / Richard Mark Friedhoff, Mark S. Peercy.
      p. cm.
    Includes bibliographical references and index.
    ISBN 0-7167-5059-7
     1. Visual programming (Computer science) I. Peercy, Mark S. II. Title.

    QA76.65. F75 2000
    005.1'18--dc21

                        00-021711

Printed in the United States of America

First printing 2000

Scientific American Library
A division of HPHLP
New York

Distributed by W. H. Freeman and Company
41 Madison Avenue, New York, NY 10010
Houndmills, Basingstoke RG21 6XS, England

This book is number 70 of a series.

*For my Family and my Friends and Colleagues
at the Rowland Institute for Science—RMF*

For Shellie and Nathan—MSP

CONTENTS

THE SOUL NEVER THINKS WITHOUT AN IMAGE

As sight is the most highly developed sense, the name
Phantasia [imagination] has been formed from Phaos [light]
because it is not possible to see without light.
—Aristotle, *On the Soul*

Visual perception requires integrating the elements of an image into objects and segregating objects from their backgrounds. This process involves making global operations across visual space to allow us to link partially occluded contours, or to interpret nuances of color and brightness to determine the shapes of objects. The ability to do this depends on more than the local physical characteristics of objects that are fed from the eyes to the visual cortex. Rather, we compare and integrate information across disparate regions of visual space. We also rely heavily on internal representations of the visual world that are embedded in our brains. These

Torsten N. Wiesel is former President and Professor of Neurobiology at The Rockefeller University. His collaborative research with David Hubel on the functional organization of the visual cortex has had a broad impact on the field of neuroscience. Among many other honors, he shared the Nobel Prize for Medicine with Hubel in 1981.

representations exert a strong top-down influence on the way we interpret scenes. The visual system is an extraordinarily efficient organ for processing vast amounts of information rapidly and in parallel. Our experience of natural scenes, the interaction between three-dimensional structure of objects, their surface qualities, and the light emitted from them, enables us to interpret complex images.

In *Visual Computing,* Richard Mark Friedhoff and Mark S. Peercy show how computer-generated images can tap into this capacity of our visual system to visualize information that would otherwise require conscious effort. The importance of visual imagery in abstract thought has been recognized for centuries. Aristotle understood the linkage between vision and imagination, having stated that "the soul never thinks without an image." Visual imagery can provide the basis for the most abstract thinking. Albert Einstein used spatial imagery in developing his theories, and analysis of his brain suggests that the most developed regions were areas of the parietal cortex that are known to be involved in perceiving spatial relationships.

Our visual system is continually adapting to the new images we are exposed to throughout life. Through a process known as perceptual learning, we embed the icons of daily life into our brains so that we can recognize them effortlessly. We can read a page of text rapidly, even though there are thousands of individual characters on that page. The properties of neurons at early stages in visual processing may be shaped to accommodate the symbols that we process preattentively. As Friedhoff and Peercy have persuasively shown, the use of computer images may create a new kind of synergy between our brains and computers. On the one hand, the computer images attempt to make use of the tricks our brains use to enable us to see. On the other hand, our visual systems, when exposed to computer images, will adapt to the three-dimensional forms they present, and learn to assimilate these images automatically and with ease. This will not turn us all into Einsteins, but it may free us for higher levels of abstract thought.

Torsten Wiesel, M.D., F.R.S.
The Rockefeller University

ILLUMINATING A REVOLUTION

The representation which a painter has to give to the light
and colors of his object I have described as a translation,
and . . . as a general rule, it cannot give a true copy in all
its details. . . . It is not the color of the objects, but the
impression which they have given, or would give, which is
to be imitated.

—Helmholtz, *On the Relation of Optics to Painting*

This ambitious book investigates a profound technological revolution
that is changing the way we work, play, communicate, and indeed,
with the emergence of the World Wide Web, the very fabric of our society. Computer games, computer-generated movies, and graphical interfaces that control our desktop computers and make it possible to surf the Internet have all been enabled by a new kind of computing that is visual. But, like most technologies that are widely adopted, visual computing has been taken for granted, and hence, not properly understood.

What is particularly enjoyable about this book is that it goes beyond the technology of visual computing and weaves lessons from art history and the science of perception to illuminate this revolution.

There is little doubt that computer graphics researchers have been strongly influenced by the observational prowess of famous artists as they uncovered the principles of naturalistic and illusionistic art. Indeed, a fair portion of the history of computer graphics can be told as the translation of the techniques of art into algorithms, software, and even hardware.

Patrick M. Hanrahan is a professor of Computer Science and Electrical Engineering at Stanford University. His work on a variety of fundamental problems in visual computing has helped establish the field as we know it today. Among his many honors are a SIGGRAPH Computer Graphics Achievement Award and a Scientific and Technical Academy Award.

The authors describe Brunelleschi's famous experiments with perspective and how his discoveries were put into practice by Renaissance painters and, much later, applied to the new field of computer graphics. They also discuss different methods painters interested in naturalism have developed to depict light and shading.

Although the development of visual computing recapitulates art history, it is not a simple reencoding of past knowledge. A painter creates the illusion of space and light by placing colors directly on a two-dimensional canvas. The big breakthrough in computer graphics, in contrast, was separating picture making into a modeling phase that builds an internal representation of a scene, and a rendering phase that converts this representation to a picture. A modern visual artist only indirectly affects an image by manipulating symbolic representations using the computer. In addition, programming a computer requires absolute precision and every case must be carefully specified: mathematically and algorithmically; efficiency is often a key issue because every calculation is repeated millions or billions of times. *Visual Computing* covers the techniques unique to this new field that are used to model light and surface in the computer, which are quite different from the classic artistic techniques.

A second major theme of the book is the importance of perception science for visual computing. At first glance, this seems obvious, considering that without our visual systems there would be no reason to make images. Our perceptual systems begin by sensing the light field that surrounds us; our brains then transform that information into our percepts. The mysterious nature of this transformation is what makes perception so fascinating. Surprisingly, perception is seldom explicitly mentioned in the classic papers of computer graphics. But do not be misled. Perception has been a key driving force behind computer graphics.

Computer scientists can find guidance in Helmholtz, one of the greatest of all perceptual scientists, who described the relationship between perception and art in a famous essay. No painter simply captures light on his canvas. Instead, the artist observes nature and adjusts the painting until it looks right; until the impression of the painting conveys his perception of the scene. Even if he does not understand scientifically the precise reasons for his adjustment, this method will lead to good results in the hands of a skilled painter. I think this is essentially the process that has been undertaken by computer graphics researchers over the last thirty years. Many computational experiments have been performed, and those that work—that is, those that give the right visual impression—have become the core techniques in the field.

As Richard Mark Friedhoff and Mark S. Peercy observe, the true subject of these experiments can be seen as the conjoined perceiver and computer. Information processing is taking place on both sides of the visual interface: the computer is executing billions of calculations to form an image, and the human visual system is performing a massive computation to interpret the image and feed its results to higher levels of cognition. This observation is extremely important because it provides insight into how the visual computer can be used to shift some of the information processing tasks in a problem to the early visual system. Not only does this help explain the value of scientific visualization, but also the success of the graphical interface and its contribution to the transformation of communication with the World Wide Web.

This book captures the current state of the art in visual computing and also points to the future. We live in a world filled with information, and it is ever more important to make it easier to navigate and understand. As we better understand perception, art history, and computing, we will be able to make more effective pictures, and we will also better understand the current explosion of myriad new forms of visual expression and communication.

Pat Hanrahan
Stanford University

PREFACE

In the late 1970s, there were just a few places in the world—no more than twenty or thirty—where the field of computer graphics was taking shape. These were mostly government laboratories, where graphics was being used to simulate nuclear explosions, for example, or to model high-energy physics. To simulate these processes required the supercomputers of the time, and even to create images representing the computations required very powerful mainframe computers. Work of this kind was being attempted only at such rarefied research establishments as Los Alamos National Laboratory, the Jet Propulsion Laboratory (JPL), and Lawrence Livermore National Laboratory.

Shortly thereafter, I was working for the Polaroid Corporation, and Dr. Edwin H. Land, founder of Polaroid and inventor of instant photography, asked me to find out why people were using instant film to take color images of computer screens. Little did I know that I was about to encounter the beginnings of an incredible revolution in technology—a revolution that ultimately transformed the Internet, by making it visual, into a worldwide communications phenomenon.

Equipped with a generous travel budget, I visited most of the places in the world where scientists were using computers to make images. Because of security restrictions, the scientists spoke only in general terms about something called "scientific visualization." But they made a compelling case for how computer visualization was enabling them to explore phenomena that would otherwise be unfathomable.

While at the Jet Propulsion Laboratory in Pasadena, California, I met an artist who had obtained permission to create artworks with JPL's computers. Today, when visual computing is ubiquitous and sophisticated

A MAN SEATED READING AT A TABLE IN A LOFTY ROOM
Follower of Rembrandt (circa 1631–1650).

interactive graphics are easily created on desktop computers, it is difficult to imagine how intriguing this creative process was.

The pictures were unique and fascinating. Using the most advanced computers available at that time, the artist sculpted columns and spirals that appeared studded with jewels. He took me on a tour through this extraordinary three-dimensional world—a halting tour, because computers of the time were not adequate to the task of interactively rendering rich imagery from detailed, three-dimensional structures. We had to wait while the computer sluggishly rendered each successive image. Nonetheless, the artist seemed amazingly familiar with the secret alleys and cul-de-sacs in his invented environment as he jumped from one position to another. Slow the process might have been, but the images revealed a world created entirely from the imagination. These were not just two-dimensional images but views of a place that paradoxically seemed real, because it was three-dimensional and we could move within it, though it existed only in the computer.

As the tour continued, I began to realize something truly staggering. The artist was not looking at images but *through the screen* into the computer. I was seeing something revolutionary. This was not merely a way of making images but a new way to think—a very intimate way to use the tremendous visual powers of human beings to link human consciousness with the tireless and unlimited computational power of the computer. This artist, and the scientists at JPL, had become partners with the computer through visual computing in a way that had never been possible before.

As a scientist, I had often used computers. On many occasions, I had keypunched Fortran instructions onto stacks of cards and left them for overnight processing at the university computer center, but, to say the least, my consciousness never fused with those computers. On the contrary, they were extremely frustrating, and we thought of them merely as a kind of giant calculator for performing repetitive computations. This computer with a window was clearly different—and that is why I felt the premonition that this was going to be very important.

In the years since my visits to those few and far-flung birthplaces of computer graphics, the technology has proliferated wildly. It has had an impact on nearly every area of science, engineering, medicine, design, entertainment, and communication, and indeed on most human endeavors. In all these fields, it is now possible to work with a visual model on the computer as a way of developing and exploring ideas. Most recently, we have seen the emergence of a new mode of visual communication over the Internet. The Internet existed for almost thirty years before protocols were developed to communicate still and moving images and graphics. Although this enhancement was not based on any radically new technical innovation, the addition of a visual mode of communication to the Internet has created a revolution in communication that is transforming everything.

All these developments flow from the field of visual computing. In this book, Mark Peercy and I step back and assess the revolution that is underway. Drawing not only from computer science but also from vision science and art history, we try to understand the nature of visual computing and the reasons for its incredible impact.

Richard Mark Friedhoff

Light in the Computer

1

What is an image? How do pigments arranged on a canvas transport us to another place and time? The pattern of light reaching our retinas from a painting is nothing like the scene it depicts, yet in some manner, the scene and the image must be perceptually equivalent. If we were to measure the light reflected from Vermeer's *The Geographer,* with its wonderful evocation of atmosphere, mood, and character, we would find that neither the intensities nor the wavelengths have any obvious connection to any real scene. Nonetheless, Vermeer's pigments introduce us to a geographer in his study. Images speak, in some manner, the language of vision.

Fundamentally, humans are visual, with more than half the brain dedicated to the intricate processing that turns two transient, meager, retinal patterns into our stable, resplendent, three-dimensional visual world. It is an extraordinary transformation that requires powerful neuronal machinery: light projected to our eyes is processed through massive computations into an immediate and continuing experience of a world that simply seems to be out there.

Therein, in the relentless organizing of the visual system lies the deep, human imperative driving the development of the visual computer. As we shall see, by synthesizing images, we can conjoin the computer's inexhaustible power with the whole, ascending structure of visual processes and fuse the computer intimately with consciousness.

We have an interesting journey ahead of us across the interface between perceiving and computing. If computers are to be used to create images that represent the world as we see it—images closely aligned with the way we perceive—then an understanding of the interplay of light and surfaces from the standpoint of both perception and computer algorithms is fundamental. In Chapter 2, "Light and Surface," we explore some of the basic competencies of human vision, with a particular emphasis on the challenge of creating a stable world of surfaces from the transient patterns of light reaching our eyes.

In Chapter 3, "Artificial Perspective," we describe the effort of scientists to model light in the computer to create images that can be properly analyzed by the visual system. Light scattered from a surface in the natural world depends upon surface roughness and spectral absorption. Objects cast shadows. Light also reflects from surface to surface, creating endless variations in brightness and color. Traditional computer graphics involves describing the three-dimensional geometry of the objects and simulating each of these qualities of light. As a result, making realistic images is computationally demanding, particularly if the images need to be generated rapidly for an interactive experience.

An alternative to modeling three-dimensional geometry and light is the direct representation of the environment of light in the computer, which is discussed in Chapter 4, "An Infinity of Pyramids." The geometry of perspective, which computer graphics has borrowed from naturalistic painting, is built upon the concept of a visual pyramid. The visual pyramid represents a collection of light rays passing through an image plane to the eye. A particular pyramid is only one of an infinite number of possible pyramids because we are immersed in a sea of light. A photographic camera records one of these pyramids, a single image. Our retinas are presented, at each instant, with two unique pyramids, one for each eye, extracted from this environment of light. Computer scientists have developed representations of this illumination environment that enable the computer to determine the image seen from any viewpoint and viewing direction. This kind of visual computing can be seen as the ultimate photographic device with which every conceivable visual pyramid, every possible picture, is recorded.

In the 1960s and 1970s, computer scientists used a mainframe computer to generate one realistically shaded image overnight. Today, it is routine to interact in real time with computer-generated worlds. Motion picture makers also have a need for speed. They often require thousands of frames to be computed for a special-effects film sequence lasting a few minutes. Architects

New Process Makes Shaded Pictures Of Nonexistent Objects

WHITE PLAINS, N.Y., November 22, 1967—A new computer process for producing toned (shaded) pictures of any three-dimensional object has been developed by Mathematical Applications Group, Inc. (MAGI). What makes the process unique is the fact that the object being portrayed is not photographed and is not physically present during the process.

The new technique, in effect, causes a computer to simulate a camera, light sources, and the object to be pictured. MAGI believes the process is a significant advance in computer graphics and should have more important engineering, film, theatrical, medical, and military uses.

MAGI, according to Sales Manager Aristides Miliotes, is a scientific computer applications and software house with headquarters in White Plains and branch offices in Lexington, Mass. and Stockholm, Sweden. In its 18-month history, the company has grown from 3 to 35 employees. MAGI specializes in the programming of advanced scientific applications such as displays, nuclear weapon effects, shock wave phenomena, and simulation of combustion processes.

How It Works

To use the new technique, the shape of the three-dimensional object to be pictured must first be manually converted to a mathematical representation and keyed into punched cards. The object's size and shape are defined in terms of nine basic geometric forms (such as spheres, cylinders, and parallelepipeds), whose relative sizes and positions are stated in

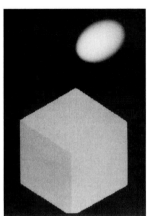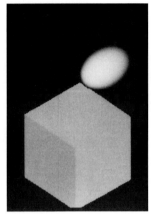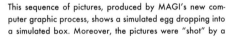

This sequence of pictures, produced by MAGI's new computer graphic process, shows a simulated egg dropping into a simulated box. Moreover, the pictures were "shot" by a simulated camera and illuminated by a simulated light source, as explained in the story.

terms of their coordinates in three-dimensional space.

Additional data describing simulated light sources and the simulated camera position and focus are also punched into cards. Then the cards are fed into a computer equipped with a special cathode ray tube whose intensity can be controlled by the stored program.

The computer traces the light rays from the simulated light sources to the simulated object, and also through the simulated camera lens to a point in the CRT. In this way, the computational process determines the light intensity at a large number of points on the tube.

The controlled-intensity rays from the CRT are then used directly to expose standard Polaroid film. The result is a fully-toned picture of the desired object, similar to one which

might be taken of an image generated by a high-resolution TV system.

According to Dr. Philip S. Mittelman, President of MAGI, the new technique should find wide application in engineering design studies, where it can eliminate the necessity for producing expensive models. Architectural designs, for example, can be visualized in three dimensions, from any specified angle and under a variety of lighting conditions.

Motion pictures can be made with the new process by producing a sequence of pictures in which the computer takes account of the motion of the various bodies, as shown in the photos. This technique should be especially useful for educational and animated cartoon films, and could eventually result in the generation of three-dimensional sets for theatrical use, with the actors actually performing on a bare stage.

The system could also help doctors by supplementing X-ray studies of internal organs, and it should aid the military in visualizing new equipment and obtaining three-dimensional views of terrain maps.

Marketing Plans

William D. Lanning, manager of MAGI's Lexington office, told COMPUTERWORLD that the new technique is now in operation on a Philco 2000 computer system in Willow Grove, Pa.

Dr. Mittelman says MAGI "expects to offer a commercially useful system within the next six months." He also notes that research is continuing, particularly in the area of color. The firm expects to be able to adapt the process so that color pictures of three-dimensional objects can be produced in addition to the black-and-white pictures now available.

LIGHT DAWNS IN THE COMPUTER This article, reprinted from a 1967 issue of *Computerworld*, is one of the first examples of modeling light in the computer. Given the then rudimentary state of computers, programmed with punch cards and having limited output devices, it is impressive that the article foresees many of the later applications of visual computing, including digital prototyping, architectural simulation, terrain simulation, medical visualization, and motion-picture special effects.

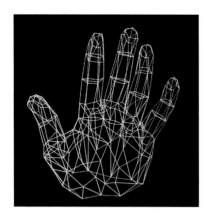

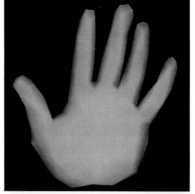

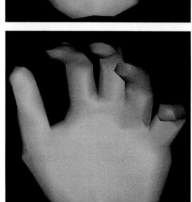

EVOLUTION OF LIGHT MODELING This series of images and the images on the opposite page depict the evolution of light modeling in the computer. These renderings of a simulated hand, milestones of computer graphics, are frames from an animation made in the early 1970s. The geometry of the hand was made by determining the spatial coordinates of points on a physical model and then connecting them with lines to form polygons as shown in the first image. As can be seen, light in these early computer graphics images was often modeled as a single, distant source reflecting from uniform, diffuse, colorless surfaces.

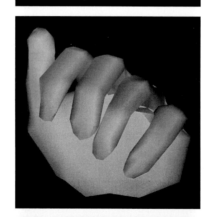

Within only a few years, computer scientists had developed rudimentary techniques to model detailed surface qualities, such as the sharp highlights of this polished metal teapot, the transparency of this wine glass, and the wrinkled surface of this orange. Light sources were still located at a distance.

During the 1980s, computer scientists greatly accelerated the drive toward realism. Here, the computer models multiple local light sources, spotlights, and cast shadows. In addition, it more faithfully models the photographic process by simulating motion blur. Motion blur is the tendency of an object to appear fuzzy in a photograph if it moves while the camera shutter is open; it is seen in the movement of the smaller lamp.

The computer can now model even the subtlest characteristics of light, such as soft shadows, area light sources, and the reflection of light from surface to surface. Virtually any illumination or surface qualities can be simulated, and the imagery made possible by the computer is limited only by the user's imagination.

may wish to give clients spontaneous tours through their designs. All of these tasks are computationally demanding. To carry them out, computer scientists have had to develop ingenious algorithms, discussed in Chapter 5, "A Sorcerer's Apprentice," where the computer acts as a creative partner to model the intricate geometric and illumination details of the natural world.

Our discussion of vision focuses on intriguing properties of human perception that are relevant to the work of artists as well as computer scientists concerned with making images. Our visual system creates a re-markable perceptual world that we enjoy with no direct awareness of the massive, neuronal processing that is occurring continuously. In Chapter 6, "Beyond Appearances," we observe that the particular competencies of *preconscious* processes, when compared with conscious processes, can be exploited to solve challenging problems. Visualization, a subfield of visual computing, is a way of making pictures from data that engage pre-conscious processes effectively. The data may originate in a computer model or it can be obtained empirically. Visualization has been used to represent thunderstorms, astrophysical black holes, the flow of air over an airplane wing, and endless other scientific, medical, engineering, and de-sign concepts.

When the field of visual computing was new, it was often said that mak-ing pictures is a good way to understand large volumes of data, because "a picture is worth a thousand words." Another common explanation of the value of visualization is that the information-carrying capacity of the visual system, its *bandwidth,* is greater than that of any other sense. Advocates of vi-sualization often pointed out that the data used to make a one-minute com-puter graphics animation might, as printed numbers, occupy a warehouse full of stacked paper, data that would be completely unfathomable in that form.

In retrospect, these older explanations seem tautological—they merely say that visualization is effective because it is effective. Furthermore, the bandwidth explanation sounds suspiciously "homuncular." We all learned in freshman psychology to avoid homunculus explanations—explaining a phenomenon by attributing it to "a little man inside." If bandwidth is the information-carrying capacity of a channel, where does the channel (and all of the information it is carrying) go? Bandwidth to where?

Since then, we have come to appreciate that the eye and brain do not merely absorb visual data at a fast rate but that visualization actually changes the information-processing strategy used to solve a problem. As described in Chapter 7, "Conscious and Preconscious," the information-

processing challenge is shifted from one part of the brain to another, from the parts of the brain concerned with conscious thinking to areas that are preconscious, hardwired to process visual information.

AN INTIMATE FUSION

Vision scientists are learning more and more about how vision works. Vision is actually a cluster of interrelated subsenses that work together to create the visual world we experience. Motion, depth, color, texture, and other properties of the visual world derive from specialized processes that work relentlessly, quickly, and in parallel to create a stable visual world from the shifting light that reaches the retinas.

When a problem is visualized, information-processing tasks are moved from the part of the brain handling serial, conscious thinking to these highly parallel *preconscious* visual processes. Preconscious is not to be confused with *unconscious*, in the sense familiar to the psychoanalytic culture.

SEEING MATHEMATICS This sequence of images shows the solution to a challenging topological problem, how a sphere can be turned inside out by stretching and passing through itself without creasing or tearing its surface. Initially, the outside surface of the sphere is gold and the inside is purple; at the end of the process, the outside is purple and the inside is gold. It would be much more difficult to understand this process through words or mathematical equations alone. The animation uses visual competencies to convey a concept that is difficult to grasp by other means.

Rather, the term "preconscious" refers to the hardwired, highly parallel processes that handle the initial stages of analysis of the retinal patterns.

An example of using visualization to shift an information-processing challenge from consciousness to preconscious competencies is the volume visualization of computed tomography (CT) data. Computed tomography produces two-dimensional images that are cross sections, for example, of the brain. In order to assess the CT scan—for example, to recognize a brain tumor—a physician would typically rely upon his or her visual imagination to create a three-dimensional mental model from the series of images. When we visualize in this way, we often say that we are "picturing something in the mind's eye."

With computer visualization, however, the physician can take the data used to make the individual images and stack them to create a three-dimensional computer model of the data. Computer graphics rendering, the modeling of the interplay of light and surfaces, can then be used to create an image. As a result of illuminating the CT scans with this "light in the computer," perhaps even rotating the model, the physician can perceive the three-dimensional structure of a patient's brain *instantly* using preconscious competencies. That part of the problem, constructing a three-dimensional structure from two-dimensional slices, has been moved from conscious thinking to the computer. The computer visualization permits the physician to use the powerful preconscious machinery of the visual system instead of conscious thinking to detect the lesion. Conscious thinking can then be focused on making the diagnosis.

In virtually all applications of visual computing, whether it is designing a building, analyzing air flow over an airplane wing, creating a textile, or modeling a black hole, a similar shift of information processing occurs from conscious to preconscious. It is also why people prefer graphical interfaces to alphanumeric ones on their personal computers. Typing alphanumeric commands interrupts the train of conscious thought, while moving and clicking a mouse uses quite separate preconscious visual and motor competencies that do not interrupt thinking. Here again, a task has been moved from conscious to preconscious. Indeed, this quality of redeploying human information-processing competencies is a driving force of the visual computing revolution.

In examining the fusion of mind with machine achieved with visual computing, it is exhilarating to think about the complementary kinds of processing that are simultaneously occurring on the two sides of the interface. On the machine side, silicon and algorithms are used to simulate light and surface

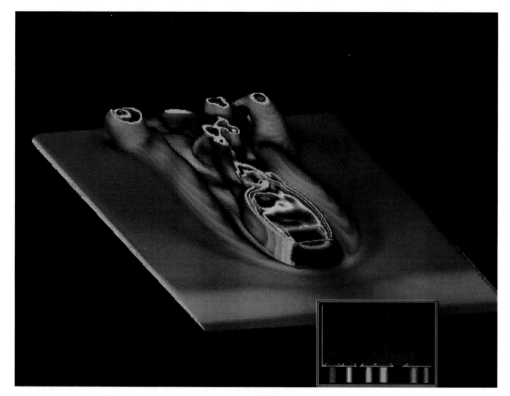

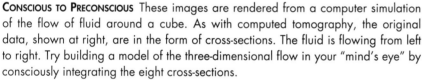

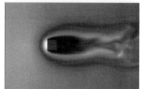

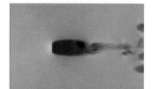

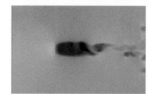

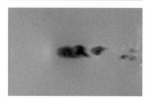

CONSCIOUS TO PRECONSCIOUS These images are rendered from a computer simulation of the flow of fluid around a cube. As with computed tomography, the original data, shown at right, are in the form of cross-sections. The fluid is flowing from left to right. Try building a model of the three-dimensional flow in your "mind's eye" by consciously integrating the eight cross-sections.

A better alternative is to use a visual computer to stack the cross-sections and render the data as a volume. In the visualization above, the gray values on the right are mapped to the color scale shown in the legend. Key values are colored and others are made transparent. The fluid is flowing from front to back. The resulting image shows the structure of the flow in three dimensions, in a form that can be perceived preconsciously. This shift from conscious to preconscious processing is characteristic of nearly every form of visual computing, from the use of graphical interfaces to the visualization of recondite scientific phenomena.

in a way that will engage the user's visual preconscious. On the human side, the pattern created by the machine is analyzed by preconscious processes that begin in the retina and ascend through highly developed structures to produce the rich and incomparable visual world we see before our eyes.

In the chapters that follow, we will move back and forth across the interface between human and machine. In so doing, we are exploring a human imperative that is not only shaping computing but also, to a great extent, our future.

Light and Surface

2

[W]hile form is absolute, so that you can say at the moment
you draw any line that it is either right or wrong, colour is
wholly relative. Every hue throughout your work is altered
by every touch that you add in other places; so that what
was warm a minute ago, becomes cold when you have put a
hotter colour in another place, and what was in harmony
when you left it, becomes discordant as you set other
colours beside it; so that every touch must be laid, not with
a view to its effect at the time, but with a view to its effect
in futurity, the result upon it of all that is afterwards to be
done being previously considered.

—*John Ruskin*

FROM PIGMENT TO LIGHT Even with its
faded colors, this detail from a painting excavated at Pompeii illustrates
that human beings are exquisitely sensitive to qualities of illumination. In this
case, the unknown artist used a variety of pigments to try to simulate the
complex interaction of direct sunlight
and ambient skylight with a variety of
colored surfaces. The effect, as we
can see at a glance, is only partially
successful. Later artists, particularly
those of the Renaissance, would develop and codify better techniques.
Even now computer scientists are challenged to invent computational methods for creating images in which light
and surface appear realistic.

To achieve the illusion of visual reality with computers has not been
easy. Looking back, one sees a remarkable evolution in visual computing that mimics, in its own peculiar way, the history of the visual arts.
Throughout history, going back to cave dwellers, artists have developed
techniques that transform pigments with the magic of alchemy. They may
not have thought of their achievements as conjuring, but a painting is first
and foremost an illusion. By some means, the artist has triggered mechanisms of perception. From mere pigment the painter can produce, in the

mind of the perceiver, not only gold, but nature and life itself. The painting, in some manner, reaches into the generative and synthesizing powers of vision and captures, if only momentarily, the attention and even the will of the viewer. The painter's techniques, if we can overcome their power and see them for what they are, are inventions that belong to the school of Merlin.

The art historian E. H. Gombrich terms the painter's representational skills, invented by artists and passed from generation to generation, visual schemata. Schemata, in Gombrich's view, transcend their application by artists and become part of humanity's shared visual vocabulary—the way that we see and understand the visual world. The short history of visual computing shows advancements that parallel those of painters, discoveries translated into algorithms, our own version of Gombrich's schemata that impart some of these same powers of illusion to visual computing.

These attempts to synthesize naturalistic images with a computer, while technically belonging to the discipline of visual computing, can also be seen as experiments in perception. In the end, an image is verisimilar only if it has been synthesized in a manner consistent with the way that we see. Thus, before we immerse ourselves in the techniques of visual computing, we will examine, in this chapter, some aspects of human visual perception and consider how several painters, in earlier epochs of art history, learned to speak the language of vision.

LIGHT AND THE PAINTER

The painting on page 10, the excavated work of an unknown Pompeiian artist, demonstrates that the challenge to faithfully render the play of light across a scene is certainly not new. This landscape depicts a solitary human figure, structures, grazing animals, and dramatic mountains. Although our eyes tell us in an instant that the play of light in the painting does not look quite right, the artist's use of many different kinds of pigments to create the illusion of a consistent interplay between light and shadow must still be admired. It is not easy to find the right mix of pigments to represent the interplay between the direct, yellowish sunlight and the ambient blue sky light as they fall upon so many different colored surfaces. Despite the passing of millennia, and inevitable changes in the pigments, present-day viewers of the artwork can still appreciate the ancient painter's struggle to understand this aspect of illusion. This painter

MADONNA AND CHILD WITH SAINTS JOHN THE BAPTIST AND MARY MAGDELENE (CIRCA 1495) Cennino Cennini in his seminal *Craftsman's Handbook* suggests a technique for reproducing the play of light over surfaces. A tonal scale is made by diluting a saturated color with white. The brightest parts of a surface are painted with the lightest tint, while the most saturated mixtures are used in the shadowed areas. Cennini's technique was an important attempt to codify a means for depicting light but, as Martin Kemp, at the University of St. Andrews, observes Cennini's schema is not entirely successful. The flat quality of the colors in this painting by Andrea Mantegna, following Cennini's prescription, are attributable to the fact that light behaves in a much more complicated manner than Cennini's schema allows. Visual computing requires computer scientists to revisit the problems of light depiction traditionally studied by painters. Modeling light in the computer, which requires formal mathematical descriptions of the behavior of light, has enlarged our understanding of the true complexity of the illumination environment.

recognized that every shadow had to be painted with a different pigment, though he was unable to unite the variety of colored shadows in a convincing manner.

Later artists devised their own strategies to address this problem. Cennino Cennini, the Italian painter (1370–1440), held a specific notion of how to depict shadows. He invented a schema that, however imperfect, could render somewhat more convincingly the interplay of light and surface. To paint a red robe, for example, he proposed that painters simply add varying amounts of white to red in three separate bowls. The mixtures were to be used as a *tonal scale* from dark to light, with pure black or white used to create the darkest or lightest surfaces, respectively.

Many artists followed Cennini's schema in the fifteenth century, but his approach proved unsatisfying because the color reflecting from the surface of a diffuse material such as cloth changes in a more subtle way as the eye moves from directly illuminated regions into areas in shadow. The light directly illuminating the subject can be quite different from the ambient illumination. This difference, which is evident in the distinct spectra of sunlight and skylight, creates endless variations that are difficult to simulate with pigment. Leonardo da Vinci, for one, spent countless hours studying fabrics draped over clay figures to try to investigate how painters could best imitate the play of light over a surface. Light is the true subject of his studies, executed in black and white with the point of a brush. His techniques when executed in frescoes and panels reveal a greater subtlety and exactness in the rendering of light and shadow than could be produced by the Cennini method.

The challenge of rendering the play of light with pigments is evident if we measure the tonal range Leonardo used to depict a uniformly colored cloth. The series of squares from light to dark on page 15 are details from Leonardo's study. Seen in context, as we inspect the painting as a whole, the cloth is perceived as a single color. In isolated details, however, parts of the representation of the cloth are dark and others are very light. Note that an almost pure black can give the appearance of a light shade.

This simple experiment, of isolating patches of Leonardo's drapery study, hints at the idea, now beginning to be embraced in vision science, that there is no perception of a surface without some corresponding and complementary perception of light. The amount of light reaching our eyes from a point in a scene depends upon both the quantity of

LEONARDO'S LIGHT The squares on the left, details from this drapery study by Leonardo da Vinci, illustrate that the perceptual separation of light and surface is based on a spatial analysis. Leonardo used a range of pigments to depict a cloth that is perceived as a uniform color. Isolated from the overall image, the same pigments are perceived to vary from nearly black to nearly white. The painting as a whole, however, creates the impression of a drapery of a single surface color with folds and shadows.

illumination and the reflective properties and orientation of the surface. The light reaching our eyes, therefore, has illumination and reflectance components that are combined. Our eyes and brains are able to factor this product into separate components of light and surface. As our exercise with Leonardo's drapery demonstrates, a black pigment may in fact depict a light surface. Leonardo has successfully provided the cues, using only pigments, for the eye and brain to build separate but complementary worlds of light and surface.

Details of Leonardo's drapery study suggest that the eye and brain do not process visual information point by point. Rather the visual system uses a spatial analysis to disentangle surface from illuminant. Indeed, in our experiment with the drapery, the small detail from the painting no longer represents the cloth and reverts to black pigment because we have destroyed the context Leonardo so convincingly constructed; we have eliminated spatial information processed by the eye and brain.

LIGHTNESS AND COLOR

In modern vision science, the notion that the lightness or darkness of a surface is dependent upon a spatial analysis of the larger scene is most forcefully represented by the work on color vision carried out by the scientist and inventor Edwin H. Land, who is well known as the creator of the instant camera. First put forward in the 1950s, Land's sometimes controversial theory of color perception, developed with John McCann, his associate at the Polaroid Corporation, fundamentally challenged some of the basic tenets of the prevailing color vision orthodoxy. Before Land, the science of color vision had been shaped by Thomas Young (1773–1829) and Hermann Ludwig Ferdinand von Helmholtz (1821–1894), who first proposed that the eye is sensitive to three separate bands of wavelengths. Both Young and Helmholtz were attempting to explain the phenomenon of color primaries: the idea, well known to painters, that a rich gamut of colors can be made from just three subtractive or additive primaries. With only this psychophysical evidence and lacking any physiological support, both Young and Helmholtz proposed that the eye is sensitive to long (red), medium (green), and short (blue) wavelengths. More recently, it has been confirmed from physiological studies that color vision is, in fact, mediated by three types of retinal receptors, called *cones*.

The Young-Helmholtz theory, also known as tristimulus theory, explains the existence of *metamers,* stimuli that are made up of different wavelengths yet produce identical color sensations. A spot of pure yellow light, for example, will stimulate the red and green cones equally, because the wavelength of yellow light lies between red and green. According to tristimulus theory, however, a spot constituted of equal parts red and green light will produce the same sensation of yellow because that spot too will equally stimulate the red and green receptors. The *red light + green light = yellow light* experiment works, and tristimulus theory goes a long way to explaining the phenomenon of color mixing. In essence, tristimulus theory says that the color perceived at a point is determined by the ratio of long, medium, and short wavelengths reflected from that point, which produce a proportional response in the three types of cones. Indeed, color photography, color printing, and color television are all based on the fact that a rich gamut of colors can be created from three well-chosen primary colors.

Mixing Red and White

Land, however, showed that there are some rather surprising exceptions to tristimulus theory that need to be reckoned with. He performed a series of experiments that contradicted the idea that colors are the result of simply adding the responses of receptors. In a now-classic demonstration of anomalies in color perception, he made two black-and-white photographic transparencies of a bowl of fruit, one through a red filter and the other through a green filter. A red apple, for instance, would appear light in the transparency taken through the red filter and dark in that taken through the green filter. Conversely, green grapes would appear dark when photographed through the red filter and light when photographed through the green filter. A yellow banana would appear nearly the same shade of gray in both transparencies.

Land then recombined the black-and-white images by projecting the first transparency through the same red filter and projecting the second transparency on top of the first without any filter at all. Since each point in the final image was a combination of red and white, tristimulus theory predicted that a variety of pinks would result from combining red and white in various proportions. Surprisingly, the projected image showed a resplendent array of colors, quite similar to a traditional color transparency, even including greens and blues.

The results were so surprising that some skeptics, who had not witnessed the great vividness of the phenomenon, suggested that the colors were the result of psychological suggestion. Critics reasoned that the colors were vague and that the observers simply imagined the familiar colors of the fruit. Land quickly eliminated this possibility by painting the bananas red, the grapes yellow, and the apples green and making a new set of transparencies. Projected only with red and white light, the painted colors were perceived correctly—for example, the atypically colored bananas were seen as red.

The key to Land's demonstrations was that he was projecting *images*. Ordinarily, red and white cannot be mixed as overlapping spots in any combination to produce green, brown, yellow, or the other colors seen in Land's red-and-white projection—only pink. Land concluded that the human visual system interprets wavelengths differently when they are used to illuminate images than when they are combined as spots of light as had traditionally been done in most color science experiments.

Land then initiated a series of experiments, using a specially invented device that enabled him to vary the wavelengths with which he would project the two photographic records of a scene. He wanted to identify the wavelengths necessary to produce a colorful scene. To everyone's surprise, he found that almost *any* two wavelengths may be used—even two green wavelengths that are nearly indistinguishable. A photographic record taken through a red filter and a green filter gives a resplendently colorful image when projected through two nearly identical green filters.

Significantly, if one removes the transparencies from the two projectors and introduces step filters in their place, the projection returns to the colors predicted by tristimulus theory. A step filter is simply a transparency in which a series of strips increase opacity from light to dark. If

COLOR FROM RED AND WHITE Traditional tristimulus theory predicts that combinations of red and white will produce only various shades of pink, and indeed this is the case if red and white spots of light are combined. When a red projected *image* is combined with a white projected *image*, however, a scene is reproduced with a full range of colors including green, yellow, blue, purple, and brown from the original scene. The top image is the black and white photographic record of a collage of colored papers exposed through a green filter. The middle image is the photographic record of the collage taken through a red filter. When the green record is projected without a filter and the red record is projected through a red filter, colors very close to those shown in the bottom full-color photograph snap into place as soon as the images are superimposed.

one step filter in one of the projectors is rotated 90 degrees to the other, a checkerboard of squares is projected, each representing a different ratio of light from the two projectors. The red-and-white projection of the two step filters produces only shades of pink. Similarly, the green-and-green projection of the step filters produces only shades of green. The step filters do not produce a range of colors the way the photographic transparencies do. Clearly, there is information in the natural scene that is used for color perception but that is not present when the pair of images is replaced with step filters. The eye and brain must be using, in contradiction to classical tristimulus theory, more than the ratios of wavelengths at a given point in the image to produce the sensation of color.

Land proposed two ideas that were radical departures for color theory. The first idea was that the eye and brain process the entire image within each waveband before the perception of color takes place. Instead of combining the responses of long, medium, and short receptors for each point in the image, as tristimulus theory asserts, the eye and brain analyze the long, medium, and short images separately. Land's concept, an idea that speaks to the whole question of understanding the play of light across a scene, is that these separate systems each produce a value for the *lightness* of each surface within the individual wavebands. The second idea was that these three lightness values determine the perceived color.

Intensity, Reflectance, and Lightness

Before going further, the terms *intensity, reflectance,* and *lightness* as they are used in vision science need to be defined. *Intensity* is simply the quantity of light that returns from a given surface. It is a physically definable value that can be measured by a photometer—a light meter. The *reflectance* of a surface is also a value that can be defined physically as the tendency of a surface to reflect light. The intensity of the light returning from an object will change as the illumination changes, whereas the reflectance will remain constant.

What is lightness? It is not a physical value, but the end product of a visual computation. It is not the same as surface reflectance. Reflectance is defined by physicists as the surface's ability to reflect light across all wavelengths, but the human eye is sensitive only to three wavebands. Furthermore, lightness is inferred from the intensities reaching the eyes but, at best, can only be an estimate of surface reflectance. It may be preferable to think of lightness as a relatively stable property of a surface independent of illumination that is unique to perception.

To understand the difference between intensity, reflectance, and lightness, consider an experiment involving a lump of chalk and a piece of black velvet. Both are suspended on hidden stands and separately illuminated by spotlights in an otherwise darkened room. If the spotlight on the black velvet is turned up sufficiently and the spotlight on the chalk is turned very low, the black velvet can be made to return more light to your eyes than the chalk. Although the chalk has a higher reflectance, in this case it has a lower intensity. Similarly, although the velvet has the lower reflectance it is actually reflecting a greater absolute quantity of light. If both objects are measured with a photometer and the reader of the measurements knows nothing about the special illumination of the scene, the higher reading on the black velvet will suggest that the object being measured is instead the white chalk. The lower reading on the chalk will suggest that the object measured is the velvet.

If you observe this demonstration with your eyes instead of the photometer, however, you will correctly perceive the chalk as white and the velvet as black even if you cannot see the source of the illumination. Your eye and brain are, in some manner, able to infer something like reflectances, the lightnesses, of surfaces even when the intensities are quite misleading. The visual system is making an estimate of the reflectance of the surface, an estimate we call *lightness,* by interpreting the image intensities in some manner.

The difference between surface reflectance and lightness also can be observed in a simple demonstration created by Alan Gilchrist of Rutgers University. A subject is placed in a completely darkened room. A card is turned forward so that it suddenly comes into view, out of the blackness, looking white as snow. Then a second card is turned forward, next to the first. At that point, the second card appears to be pure white and the first instantly takes on a slightly grayish appearance. When a third card is revealed, the second card becomes a shade of gray and the first a still darker shade. This process continues through a total of twelve cards aligned in a row, with the new card always seeming to be pure white and the other cards darkening. At the end, when the lights in the room are finally turned on, one sees that the first card is actually black, and that the last card is the only truly white card. All the cards in between are steps from black to white.

In Gilchrist's demonstration, the first card initially appears to be white, but is black. The visual system estimates the reflectance to be high, but it is actually low. This difference illustrates that it is necessary to have separate terms, reflectance and lightness, for the actual and perceived value. Gilchrist's demonstration also suggests something about the limitations of the method by which the eye infers reflectances. In some sense, the eye and brain require information from more than a single surface in the scene to produce a reliable estimate of reflectance. In the absence of other surfaces, the lightest surface in this simplified environment is assumed to be white, to have a high reflectance. This is true even if the only visible surface is coal black, as was the case with the first card.

From Intensity to Lightness

The question arises as to how the leap is made from intensity to lightness—what neural computation underlies an estimate of reflectance from the intensities that reach the eyes? As amply demonstrated by the example of the white chalk and the black velvet, reflectance based on intensity can be completely wrong when the illumination is unevenly distributed.

At first glance, particularly if you consider only individual points, obtaining reflectance from intensity might seem like an unsolvable problem. On the other hand, consider that intensity and reflectance *are* perfectly correlated as long as the illumination is evenly distributed across the scene. If the light is perfectly even, with no shadows and no bright spots, a surface with a high reflectance will return proportionately more light to your eyes than a surface with a low reflectance. Therefore, to make the leap back to reflectance from intensity when the illumination is uneven, spatial changes in the illumination must be disregarded.

Land and McCann developed a mathematical procedure, an algorithm, that accounts for spatial changes in the illumination with some success. Their algorithm is based on the idea that changes in illumination are somewhat more gradual than changes in surface reflectance. This is, in fact, often the case because surface color changes abruptly at the edges of objects. Spatial changes in illumination—for example, shadows—are more likely to create soft transitions between light and dark. In essence, implementing the Land-McCann algorithm is similar to moving a photometer from area to area within an image plane. Abrupt transitions are assumed to be surface reflectance changes, while soft transitions are disregarded. Unless, for some reason, an illumination and reflectance transition coincide, this technique will yield relative values for reflectance for all the surfaces in the scene. In order to turn relative reflectances into estimates of absolute reflectance, however, the algorithm assumes the highest reflectance in the scene to be white—an assumption that may or may not be correct.

The Land–McCann Color Theory

The idea of lightness is fundamental to the theory of color perception developed by Land and McCann. Land and McCann proposed that each of the three sensitivity systems processes the entire image separately and determines a lightness value for each surface. Since each of the three systems is sensitive to a different waveband of light, three separate reflectance estimates are generated at this early stage of visual processing: lightness values for long, medium, and short wavebands. For example, a red surface would produce a high lightness value in the long-wavelength system but a low lightness value in the short-wavelength system. Similarly, a green surface would produce a high value for lightness in the medium-wavelength system and somewhat lower values for lightness in the long- and short-wavelength systems.

According to the Land–McCann color theory, these three numbers form the perception known as color. Indeed, Land and McCann created a three-dimensional color space in which color regions are defined as triplets of lightness values. The lightness triplets for a number of different surfaces are computed with their algorithm, and the perceived colors are positioned in Cartesian space.

This approach is fundamentally different from tristimulus theory because the relative values of long, medium, and short wavelengths for a given point in the scene do not determine the perceived color or, as Land put it, "the color perceived at a point is not determined by the point." Instead, each of the three lightnesses is a product of a neural computation within a waveband, based on a large area of the scene rather than a point.

Land and McCann's theory explains how color is perceived in the red-and-white or green-and-green projections. It is possible to predict the perceived colors by calculating lightness triplets for each surface in the red-and-white projection with the Land and McCann algorithm and placing those values in the three-dimensional color space. These locations

TONE REPRODUCTION This image of the interior of Memorial Church at Stanford University has been processed to create a perception that is closer to reality than an unprocessed image. A photographic print would not be able to depict the quality of light within the church because the light has too great a dynamic range. A visitor to the church will, on the other hand, readily perceive both the dark and light areas because the human eye adjusts its sensitivity as we survey an unevenly illuminated scene. To recreate the quality of actually visiting the church in this image, several photographs were taken at different exposures to capture detail at all light levels. A technique known as *tone reproduction,* a cousin of photographic dodging and burning, was used to pool these separate photographs into a single image that can be reproduced within the limits of printing. The resulting image has the detail we would see in the darkest and lightest areas of the church and so is a better representation of the actual scene than an unprocessed image. It might be said that the adaptation of the human visual system to different light levels has been transferred to the computer.

SIMULTANEOUS CONTRAST It has long been known that there is a spatial aspect to lightness and color perception. The bar in the middle of this figure is printed with a uniform density but appears to vary from light gray to dark gray because of the changing background. A gray surface surrounded by black is perceived to be lighter than the same gray surrounded by white. Colors can actually appear to change not only lightness but also hue when placed against different backgrounds. Traditionally, these kinds of color and lightness effects are known as simultaneous contrast. The influence of neighboring colors is a considerable challenge to painters interested in faithfully reproducing surface color and in creating a convincing environment of light.

correspond roughly to those that would be found by someone looking at the scene itself, indicating that the lightness values, and hence estimates of surface reflectance, are similar in both cases. Indeed, Land built a light-measuring device that could be dragged across the red-and-white projection to feed data into a computer that would spatially compute lightness values with his algorithm. The device and computer correctly predict the perceived colors rather than shades of pink.

Land and McCann's color theory also goes a long way toward explaining the phenomenon of color constancy—the idea that colors do not change their fundamental appearance despite drastic changes in the spectral composition of the illumination. Colors retain their familiar appearance, whether we are wearing green or orange sunglasses or whether we are standing in yellow, early-morning light or blue, midday light. The lightness values within the long, medium, and short sensitivity systems are stable, despite marked changes in the light reaching our eyes, in part because the three receptor systems are each sensitive to a very broad range of wavelengths. If the three cone systems were sensitive only to narrow bands of wavelengths, even small changes of the illuminating spectra would cause dramatic differences in the computed lightnesses.

In certain kinds of illumination, however, the system malfunctions. Most of us have had the experience of trying to find a car at night in a parking lot illuminated by mercury vapor or sodium lamps. Because the lamps produce light in narrow wavebands rather than broadband illumination, the three sensitivity systems cannot make reliable estimates of lightness, and the apparent color of an automobile may be totally different from its color in daylight.

Land and McCann's theory is based upon psychophysical observations and does not really address the underlying visual physiology. Indeed, as Land and McCann were aware, long, medium, and short receptors—cones—do not connect to independent long, medium, and short visual pathways. In fact, even at the earliest stages, color is processed by neurons that oppose red and green or yellow and blue. In the first instance, red might increase the response rate of a neuron while green might suppress its rate of firing. Other neurons might respond to particular spatial relationships between red and green. Yellow and blue appear to be opposed in a similar manner, with a key difference being that there are no yellow cones. Instead, yellow is based on an input that is the sum of red and green cone inputs. There are many variations on the theme of opponency in the visual system, but the important point is that Land and McCann's original proposal regarding three separate channels needs to be reconciled with the physiological reality of red-green and yellow-blue opponency. The two theories may not be irreconcilable, however, as one kind of encoding can be transformed into the other. Since the Land color theory does a good job of predicting perceived colors, one might expect that, when more is understood about the processing of color information, Land and McCann's general approach can be fully integrated with the physiologically observed opponent organization of the visual system.

The virtues of a visual system organized in the manner suggested by Land are considerable. Objects retain their familiar appearance in a wide range of illumination environments. This type of vision should also be adaptive: despite the highly transitory nature of illumination, the world has a stable appearance.

LIGHTNESS AND THE THIRD DIMENSION

The Land-McCann algorithm works well as long as surface color and illumination do not change abruptly at the same place. The algorithm yields correct colors only if the illumination changes more gradually from point to point than does surface reflectance. In the natural world, these are serious limitations.

Consider, for example, a cube in which each of the six faces is a different color. The illumination might change sharply at the edge between one surface and another, just where the surface color also changes.

Indeed, changes at an edge in both illumination and color are common occurrences in the real three-dimensional world, where objects in the foreground may be illuminated differently from objects in the background. An image made of a three-dimensional scene is likely to include these kinds of coincident illumination and surface boundaries. Land acknowledged this limitation of the algorithm and noted that the same computational device that could be dragged across the red-and-white projection to compute lightness triplets did not work well when there were sharp shadows in the scene. Applied to a scene with concurrent surface and illumination boundaries, the Land-McCann algorithm would yield incorrect lightness values and thus map surfaces to points in their color space that do not correspond to the colors someone would actually perceive.

Another demonstration by Alan Gilchrist shows how it is sometimes difficult to reduce the computation of lightness to a two-dimensional problem. Gilchrist has created a model of two rooms with a door between them. An observer looks into these two rooms through a peephole and sees a dark square of paper hovering in the air in what appears to be the front room. The paper is actually suspended in the back room but appears to be in the front room because Gilchrist has played a trick on the viewer. He has cut out a corner of another piece of paper in the doorway between the two rooms so that the back paper appears to occlude the doorway paper. Although it is not possible to see the sources of illumination, the front room is illuminated with bright light, while the back room is illuminated at a much lower level.

Without actually moving the piece of paper, Gilchrist can make it appear to be hovering in the air in the back room. All he needs to do is remove the paper attached to the doorway. The surprising result is that, although the paper is reflecting exactly the same amount of light in both conditions, as measured by a photometer, it completely changes its lightness. When it seems to be in the front room it appears to be dark gray, but when it is judged to be in the back room it has a light gray appearance. The scene that is perceived through the peephole does not change in any manner that should change the paper's lightness value significantly as calculated by the Land-McCann algorithm. The only detail that changes is the removal of the cue that suggests that the test paper is in the front room.

Gilchrist's experiment suggests that the neural computations of the eye and brain are somehow incorporating the three-dimensional environment of light into the lightness computation. When the paper is understood to be in the front room, we perceive it as a dark piece of paper in a brightly lit environment. When the paper is understood to be in the back room, we perceive the same piece of paper, reflecting exactly the same amount of light, as a light piece of paper in a dark environment.

The importance of the three-dimensional environment of light in determining surface lightness is also evident in John Singer Sargent's painting *The Daughters of Edward Dorley Boit,* which has kinship with Gilchrist's two-room experiment. Two girls are located in a brightly lit foreground, while two others are standing in a darker middle room. In order to make

THE DAUGHTERS OF EDWARD DORLEY BOIT (1882) Psychophysicist James Schirillo of Wake Forest University has observed that this painting by John Singer Sargent is reminiscent of Alan Gilchrist's two-room experiment. The two girls depicted in the foreground are brightly lit from their right, while the girls in the back room are in shadow. Sargent used darker pigments for the pinafores in the background and lighter pigments for the pinafores in the foreground, but they all appear pure white. If one of the girls in the darker room were to step forward into the brighter room with the dress painted with the same pigments, the dress would appear to be dingy gray. Sargent's painting and Gilchrist's experiment suggest that the eye and brain, in some sense, are modeling three-dimensional qualities of light.

BUILDING AN ILLUMINATION WORLD In this figure from Edward Adelson, the region marked *a* is printed with the same ink density as that marked *c*, yet we perceive them as belonging to cubes apparently made of differently colored materials. The upper cube appears to be darker than the lower cube. These inferences about surfaces are linked to the assumption that the illumination is falling more directly on the top surface than on the front and side yet there is no real illumination—only an arrangement of dark and light patches on the page. This stimulus suggests that complementary three-dimensional models of surfaces and illumination are constructed by the eye and brain.

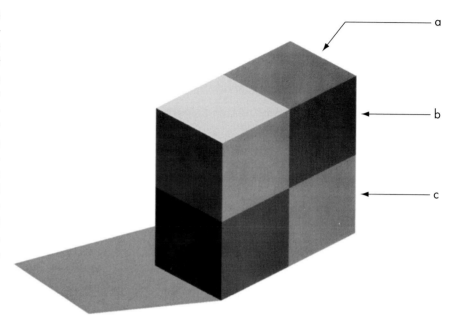

their pinafores appear to be of the same type of white linen, Sargent had to use darker pigments in the back room. There are differences in the reflectances of these pigments, yet they all appear to represent the same reflectance in the painting. Working about a hundred years before Gilchrist's demonstration, Sargent understood in artist's terms how to use pigments on a two-dimensional surface to trigger the perception of a three-dimensional environment of light.

Gilchrist's room experiment suggests that in some manner the eye and brain build a three-dimensional model of the illuminant that is a complement to the three-dimensional model of objects that we normally think of as our visual environment. Indeed, Land and Gilchrist's experiments suggest that the two worlds of light and surface can hardly exist without each other.

Edward Adelson of the Massachusetts Institute of Technology has elegantly demonstrated the complementary relationship between surface and illuminant in the simple figure on this page representing a two-by-two checkerboard arrangement of cubes. The arrangement of light and dark panels suggests that an illuminant strikes the upper surfaces more directly than the front surfaces. The area marked *a* is actually printed with the same density as the area marked *c*. Nonetheless, it appears to be the same as that marked *b,* which is printed with a greater density. The visual system assumes *a* and *b* to be two faces of a cube made from a single material, with a common reflectance. The illustration shows that intensity is not the sole determinant of lightness and suggests that lightness depends upon a three-dimensional analysis of light and surface.

In the next figure, also devised by Adelson, the three-dimensional model of the illuminant, however it is derived perceptually, can be broken up by removing cues supporting a three-dimensional perception of the object. When this is done, the lightness changes markedly. When the lower half of the figure is shifted slightly to the right, the object appears flat. Adjacent surfaces that had identical lightnesses in the apparently raised diamond have different lightnesses in the apparently flat surface. Again, assessing lightness appears to be a three-dimensional problem that includes an interpretation of the shape of the objects and the direction of the illumination.

All of this raises the question of how the eye and brain might make the leap from the two-dimensional patterns of light projected to the retina, in which surface and illuminant are confounded, to separate surface and illumination worlds. Land and McCann's algorithm encourages us to believe that this problem, which might at first glance seem unsolvable, is manageable if the scene is considered as a whole instead of point by point.

The figure on page 30, inspired by V. S. Ramachandran of the University of California at San Diego, suggests that the eye and brain

REMOVING THE ILLUMINATION WORLD The left image appears to be a raised diamond of a single lightness illuminated from above. When the lower half of this image is shifted to the right, however, the three-dimensional appearance is lost, and the resulting image appears to be a flat, herringbone pattern made up of different shades of gray. In the right figure there is no apparent source of illumination. Surfaces that have identical lightnesses in the first version have different lightnesses when the three-dimensional object appears two-dimensional. Once again there appears to be a close connection between the perception of three-dimensional objects and the perception of an illumination environment.

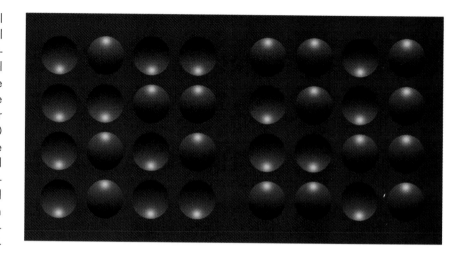

LIGHT FROM ABOVE How does the visual system build a three-dimensional model of the illumination environment? This figure suggests a partial answer. Ovals with highlights on the top half appear to be convex while those with bottom highlights appear concave. If the figure is rotated 180 degrees, however, by turning the book upside down, the convex and concave ovals reverse. The visual system apparently processes the retinal patterns as if light is coming from above. Presumably, this is an evolutionary adaptation to a world illuminated by sunlight shining from the sky. With conscious effort, one can reverse the convex and concave shapes but then the light appears to shine from below. It is not possible to switch only some of the convex or some of the concave figures. The visual system apparently makes a single, global, estimation of the lighting environment.

may make some assumptions about the direction of the illuminant that simplify the problem greatly. Notice that some of the oval shapes in Ramachandran's figure appear to be convex and others concave. If the figure is rotated 180 degrees by turning the book upside down, the formerly convex ovals appear to be concave and the formerly concave ovals appear to be convex. The figures are, in fact, ambiguous: an oval that appears concave and illuminated from above is the same as a convex surface illuminated from below. The figure suggests, therefore, that the eye and brain tend to assume that illumination comes from the top, as is usually the case with natural light. Perhaps to conform to our visual expectation, artificial lighting is often overhead, and even when lamps are used, they are generally not placed low. Although imagining a light source from the bottom can perceptually reverse concave and convex figures, it is impossible to see the oppositely shaded parts of Ramachandran's figure as simultaneously convex or concave. Apparently only one model of the illuminant is possible at a given moment.

PERCEPTION AND VISUAL COMPUTING

Some may say that an understanding of perception is not required to make images. If we could easily reproduce the exact wavelengths and intensities of the world, perception science would, it is true, be less important, at least for a time. In practice, however, the image maker, whether painter or computer scientist, is always making choices among schemata, and the choices determine the kind of visual world that can be created. More important, a fundamental understanding of the relationship between images and vision, the relationship between our imaging strategies and the responses of armies of neural processors that are the antecedent of our visual experience, makes it possible to better ally computing and human thinking.

In both naturalistic painting and visual computing, the representation of light is the first place to start to create images that fully engage visual processes. As we will see in the next chapters, a variety of strategies—computer schemata, if you will—have been developed to imitate the behavior of light, each with its advantages and limitations. If the eye and brain were less effective at untangling surface and illuminant, the challenge to computer algorithm designers would be significantly reduced. Algorithms for rendering computer graphics can be conceptually elegant but produce an image that appears artificial—and we know it at a glance.

It takes an effort of the imagination to fully appreciate that the visual world we inhabit, built only from intensities reaching the retinas, is the singular achievement of a massively powerful neural computer. Vision science makes us aware that, without the slightest conscious effort, the human visual machinery synthesizes a world that simply appears to be there.

Significantly, the light we see in this visual world is not to be confused with the raw energy that reaches our eyes, for that is only the uninformed messenger. Indeed, in a certain sense, the light measured by the physicist has never been seen by human beings. That light is a mix of reflective surface and energy that, uninterpreted, is not the visual world as we know it.

The designers of computer graphics algorithms are, perhaps without intending to do so, uncovering secrets of visual perception in their own unique language, just as painters have long done in theirs. When an algorithm produces a convincing image, a discovery has been made about two exquisitely human worlds—complementary worlds of surface and light that exist nowhere in the universe but within our perceptions.

Artificial Perspective

3

A painting is the intersection of a visual pyramid at a given distance, with a fixed center and a defined position of light, represented by art with lines and colors on a given surface.

—*Leon Battista Alberti,* On Painting

THE SCHOOL OF ATHENS The interest among Renaissance painters in the naturalistic depiction of space, form, and light may have reached its apex in the works of Raphael. His *The School of Athens,* a portion of which is shown here, is an encyclopedia of Renaissance techniques. The painting is a window opening onto space that is continuous with that of the viewer. This scientific depiction of space is now known as *perspective.* Before the Renaissance, however, the term referred more generally to geometrical theories of optics and human vision. Thus, in Raphael's time, painters would have referred to this method of painting as *artificial* perspective. The basic procedures of perspective painting are reiterated today in visual computing.

In the early fifteenth century, the Florentine architect Filippo Brunelleschi—who would design one of the engineering and artistic marvels of the Renaissance, the great dome of the Florence Cathedral—performed an experiment that quietly signaled the beginning of a revolution in the visual culture of the West. Today's computer graphics algorithm designers have much to learn from this fifteenth-century Italian artist's experiments with geometry, light, and naturalism. Indeed, it might be argued that the perspectival schemata devised for painting by Brunelleschi and other Renaissance artists provided the conceptual foundations for the later field of computer graphics.

At the time, *perspective* was a term that referred to a geometrical interpretation of vision, and Brunelleschi was attempting to apply these geometrical concepts to painting. Following a procedure that has remained unknown in its details, Brunelleschi painted an image of the Baptistry across the piazza from the Florence Cathedral, on a small panel. When the painting was finished, Brunelleschi drilled a hole in it so that peering from the back one could see the painting reflected in a mirror. The painting positioned in this manner could be directly compared to its subject. When the mirror was removed, the Baptistry took the place of the reflected painting.

Such was the faithfulness of the painting to the real scene, that it is said viewers had difficulty perceiving any difference as the mirror was removed and replaced. Although historians do not know the precise nature of Brunelleschi's technique, it was recognized at the time as a means to reproduce, in a painting, the manner in which objects change their apparent size with increasing distance from the viewer, the fundamental idea of linear perspective.

Brunelleschi's experiments inspired a proponent in the person of Leon Battista Alberti, a scholar, painter, architect, and man of letters. Impressed by the demonstration, Alberti sought to codify Brunelleschi's findings and to make them the basis of a new mode of representation. In his seminal *On Painting,* Alberti describes a method for drawing in perspective that is rigorous and systematic. Following this technique, the space depicted in the painting is continuous with that of the observer. It is a transitional moment in the history of art: a painting becomes, in essence, a window open onto the world. *On Painting* stands today as one of the most influential works in the history of painting and a defining work of the Renaissance.

Alberti devised a practical method for perspectival representation that has special significance for computer graphics. The German artist Albrecht Dürer (1471–1528) illustrated the basic technique in a series of woodcuts, one of which is shown at right. Alberti placed a fine veil with black threads woven in a grid pattern between the painter and the scene. In front of the painter, he placed a second grid. He then fixed the point of view, directing the artist's gaze through the veil. The artist then painted on the grid the colors seen through each point using the black threads and grid lines as a guide. In this manner a geometrically correct image could be created point by point.

Alberti's technique is a method for projecting the three-dimensional scene in perfect proportion onto a two-dimensional plane. A tree in the background, for instance, occupies a smaller number of grid squares than does a tree of the same size in the foreground. Thus, scale is properly determined. Alberti's methodology is based upon the notion of the vanishing point: a road extending toward the horizon will diminish until the two sides occupy the same point. Indeed, any object moved farther and farther away, will subtend a smaller and smaller region of the grid until it occupies just a single grid point.

Alberti's method, although designed to enforce geometric perspective, coincidentally determines the color for each point in the image when transcribing a real scene. The color for any point in the image plane can be determined by defining a straight line that starts at the viewpoint, passes through the image plane, and encounters a surface in the scene. Of course, as noted in the previous chapter, the color of the point on the encountered surface is not only a property of the surface itself but also a function of the illumination of the scene.

Alberti identified four elements that are reiterated in computer graphics: the scene, sources of light, a visual pyramid that is transected by a picture plane, and a station point. In computer graphics, the term *image plane* is generally preferred to picture plane, and *viewpoint* is used rather than station point. In Brunelleschi's experiment, the viewpoint is the position of the artist's eye. In Dürer's woodcut, the artist places his eye at the tip of a small obelisk on a table, fixing the viewpoint as he works. The visual pyramid is formed by extending lines from the viewpoint through the four corners of the veil, with the veil itself transecting the pyramid and defining an image plane. The scene is simply the model reclining on two

PERSPECTIVE ILLUSTRATED In this woodcut, Albrecht Dürer depicts Alberti's schema for translating points in a scene to points in a drawing. A grid, shown here in a frame, defines an image plane from a particular viewpoint, indicated by the obelisk. The artist translates details from this grid to a corresponding grid on his drawing. An image constructed in this manner faithfully reproduces the spatial relationships between objects in the scene.

pillows, and the illumination is the daylight streaming in the back windows. The light and surfaces together determine the shading and shadow that the artist seeks to replicate with paint.

In the computer, of course, objects do not exist except as mathematically defined surfaces at different positions in a simulated three-dimensional space. Likewise, surface reflectances, as well as the positions, shapes, and spectral composition of light sources, and the viewing pyramid are all described mathematically. The guideline squares in Alberti's veil are large so that whole objects in the scene may fit within a single square. The painter uses the guidelines to maintain control over relative distances and sizes of the various elements in the scene. In computer graphics, however, Alberti's large grid squares have been replaced by pixels, rectangular elements of the computer screen that are, ideally, small enough to be imperceptible. Each pixel, furthermore, has only one color. Pixel color is determined by computing the light scattered from the scene through the pixel to the viewpoint. Since this light depends upon both the objects and the illumination, a great challenge of computer graphics is to simulate with mathematics all of the nuances of the play of light on surfaces within the synthetic scene.

FROM SIMPLE TO COMPLEX: DEFINING OBJECT GEOMETRY

Before the interaction of light and surfaces can be simulated, all of the objects in the scene must be mathematically defined. Objects are defined as sets of points in three dimensions satisfying geometrical equations. Usually, the three-dimensional geometry is specified relative to a Cartesian coordinate system with three axes, x, y, and z. For example, a sphere can be described by the three-variable equation $(x - x_0)^2 + (y - y_0)^2 + (z - z_0)^2 = r^2$, where the sphere has its origin at the point (x_0, y_0, z_0) and a radius equal to r. Points whose x, y, and z values satisfy the equation form the surface of the sphere.

Typically, a computer graphics program is able to process only a relatively small number of geometric shapes. These objects, known as primitives, might include spheres, cylinders, and other forms that are easily characterized with simple mathematical formulae. Additionally, a number of points in three dimensions may be connected with lines to form the

WIREFRAME RENDERING In three-dimensional computer graphics, objects are first defined mathematically as surfaces in the computer and only later acquire more familiar visible characteristics. Even the most complex objects must be assembled, in some manner, from geometric primitives such as spheres, cylinders, polygons, and curved surface patches. Each spiral in this illustration has been made by sweeping a two-dimensional cross-section along a three-dimensional curve. The eggs and the table support have been generated by rotating a two-dimensional curve around an axis. The tetrahedra and cube are constructed from cylinders, spheres and polygons. The teapot lid is comprised of curved patches. In this simple rendering, called a wireframe, all of these surfaces have been converted to polygons and only their edges are drawn. In subsequent images in this chapter (rendered by Matt Pharr of Stanford University), these objects will be illuminated with synthetic light using various computational models.

boundaries of a *polygon,* another kind of primitive. From this toolkit of simple shapes, more complex objects are created. Even visually intricate scenes can be built up of combinations of appropriately scaled and positioned geometric primitives.

For shapes that do not lend themselves easily to geometric descriptions a *polygon mesh* may be used. A polygon mesh is a set of connected, flat polygons that are chosen to approximate the irregular geometry of a surface. The polygon mesh method works well for objects composed of flat surfaces, but it often is a poor approximation for curved surfaces. To overcome this problem, the number of polygons can be increased, or alternatively, a *parametric mesh* can be utilized. As with a polygon mesh, a parametric mesh approximates a surface by stitching together a number of smaller patches. The difference is that these patches, unlike polygons, can be curved.

While it is certainly possible to define objects by writing geometric equations for their constituent primitives in computer code, it is much more convenient to use specialized applications that provide a *graphical interface* so that objects can be generated and modified by a direct, visual interaction with the computer. These applications, known as *modelers,* make it possible to automatically generate and then visually manipulate primitives to create three-dimensional forms. A primitive can be rotated, translated, and scaled before being positioned. Custom shapes are made by modifying a primitive: a silhouette edge such as a two-dimensional curve can be rotated around an axis to create a body of rotation, a process that can be compared to lathing in woodworking. A two-dimensional cookie-cutter shape may be dragged through a path in three dimensions to create a variation of a cylinder, a process that has kinship with extrusion.

Modelers make computer graphics much more practical and make it possible to focus on design rather than on mathematics. It would be a formidable task for a designer to specify intricate objects point by point. In these methods of lathing or extrusion, for example, the computer itself is used to create surface geometry. This approach is generally known as *procedural modeling* and is essential for creating complex objects such as clouds, mountains, and trees in the computer, as we shall discover in Chapter 5, "A Sorcerer's Apprentice."

Visible Surfaces

Up to this point, we have defined the surfaces of objects only as points satisfying equations: we still have no image of the scene to view. To synthesize an image, we need to model the light falling on the scene that is reflected to the image plane. This process, known as *rendering,* involves the other three elements defined by Alberti: the viewpoint, visual pyramid, and sources of light.

The viewpoint and viewing direction are specified in the computer in the same three-dimensional mathematical space that contains the scene. The angular extent of the image measured from the viewpoint, the field of view, uniquely determines a visual pyramid. The image is a slice of pixels through this pyramid, equivalent to Alberti's veil.

Unless an object is transparent, we should see only the portion of its surface that is unobstructed from our viewpoint. The next step in rendering is, therefore, to find the surface closest to the viewpoint for each pixel in the final image. By starting at the viewpoint, we can project a ray through each pixel into the three-dimensional scene. Since both the rays and the objects are described mathematically, the points that a ray intersects can be precisely computed.

A single ray through one pixel might intersect the front and back surfaces of several objects. It might, for instance, first intersect a flat polygon and then a sphere at two points, once on the front surface and once on

LIGHT TRAVELS IN STRAIGHT LINES Four centuries before Brunelleschi and Alberti, the Arabian mathematician and physicist Alhazen (965–1039) rediscovered classical theories of optics. He challenged the orthodoxy of his day that vision is mediated by rays emanating outward from the eyes and proposed the correct view that light is reflected to the eyes from the external world. Alhazen studied the manner in which light can project an image in a *camera obscura,* a dark room with a hole in one wall that admits light. As shown in this eighteenth-century etching, the light entering the room projects an inverted image. Through his experiments with the camera obscura, Alhazen concluded that light travels in straight lines and extended this insight to the workings of the eye and a theory of vision. His ideas influenced Leonardo da Vinci and other Renaissance painters and formed the conceptual foundations for perspective painting.

the back surface. The first object intersected by the ray usually is not known beforehand, however, so the intersections with all objects may need to be computed. The visible surface is simply the intersection with the shortest distance to the viewpoint. This procedure, determining which surfaces need to be rendered, is called *hidden surface removal.* When objects are intended to be transparent, however, there are no hidden

HIDDEN SURFACE REMOVAL The computer must be instructed to render only surfaces visible from a particular perspective. In this image, occluded surfaces have been removed by identifying the surfaces that are closest to the viewpoint. Each surface is rendered with a single color and there is no illumination.

surfaces to be removed. Hidden surface removal is bypassed, and the rendered image depicts front and back surfaces.

The final step in image synthesis is the determination of the color of the visible surface represented by each pixel. This requires that the computer model the subtle interaction of all of the illuminants with surfaces.

SIMULATING LIGHT AND SURFACE

Our brief survey of some of the basic competencies of human vision suggests a certain reciprocity between computing and perceiving. Visual computing is used to synthesize an image in which light and surface are combined so that they can be later separated by vision. When all goes well, the image appears realistic.

The Envelope of Light

The development of algorithms to simulate light in the computer inevitably requires a rich education in the properties of the visual world and particularly the intricate nature of the illumination environment. In the natural world, light is composed of many different wavelengths, familiar as the visible spectrum from violet to red. A given light source will radiate

DIFFUSE REFLECTION A source of illumination has been introduced into the scene. The computer models the way in which this light reflects from each of the surfaces. In this image, the surfaces are modeled as purely diffuse reflectors. The reflected light does not depend upon the location of the viewer but only on the orientation of the surfaces with respect to the light source.

different proportions of energy at different wavelengths, the light's *spectral power distribution*. Light in a scene might emanate from multiple sources, each with its own spectral power distribution, shape, and position. For example, a small, tungsten filament emits light that consists predominantly of red wavelengths with very little energy in the blue portion of the spectrum. The small size of the filament also creates sharp shadows. Fluorescent light, on the other hand, principally comprises a small number of wavelengths of light produced by the energized gas, but it is softened by a coating that fluoresces broadly across the visible spectrum. Fluorescent lights, also in contrast to tungsten light bulbs, create very soft shadows, or *penumbrae*.

Light reflected from a surface is a product of the spectral power distribution of the illuminant and the surface reflectance.

Typically, the surface reflectance of an object changes as the orientation of the surface is altered with respect to both the illumination direction and the viewing direction. A simple experiment with a flashlight beam reflected off a flat matte board illustrates the effect of surface orientation. As the board is rotated to face your eyes or to face the flashlight, the amount of reflected light will vary, but only gradually. This type of reflection, called *diffuse reflection* (or *Lambertian reflection*, after the French mathematician who studied it, Johann Lambert, 1728–1777) is a function

SPECULAR REFLECTION Some of the surfaces in this image have been modeled to be highly reflective. The highlights result from a mirrorlike scattering of light known as specular reflection. These specular reflections have been added to the diffuse reflections of the preceding image.

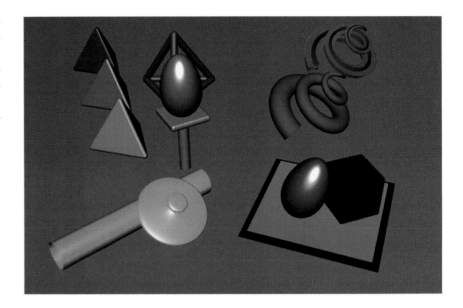

only of the angle between the light source and the reflecting surface. In diffuse reflection the angle between the reflecting surface and the viewer generally is assumed to be unimportant.

If the matte board is replaced by a mirror, however, the reflection is quite different. In this case, the flashlight beam will actually be diverted, and, at one angle, the beam will be reflected directly into your eyes. This mirrorlike type of reflection is known as *specular reflection*.

Most surfaces are neither perfectly diffuse nor perfectly specular and have some combination of the two types of reflection. For example, the red paint on a new car changes in brightness as the angle formed by the illuminant and car surface is varied. At a certain angle, it is possible to see the reflection of the light source, in a mirrorlike fashion, and difficult to see the red pigment at all. At another angle, the red pigment will be quite apparent. This combination of diffuse and specular components is quite evident in many types of materials including molded plastic, varnished wood, glossy paper, and waxy leaves. It can even be noticeable in hair and the contours of some fabrics.

Diffuse and specular reflection arise from distinct physical processes. Commonly, an object in the natural world is inhomogenous; it consists of a transparent host that carries some colorant material that selectively

SURFACE PROPERTIES In this image, the computer has employed sophisticated mathematical models to simulate the way in which light interacts with a variety of materials such as red velvet, brushed copper, and teal blue paint. Light now passes through the egg and tetrahedra. However, unlike real transparent materials, these objects do not refract light in this illumination model.

absorbs and reradiates light. Leaves, for example, obtain their color from green chlorophyll contained in cells made mostly from water. Colored plastics are created by mixing a material that absorbs or reflects the desired color in a transparent host. Paint, such as that used on the red car fender, consists of pigments or metal flakes suspended in a clear medium. Countless other materials, including varnished wood, skin, and glossy paper, are similarly inhomogenous.

Specular reflection comprises the light that is scattered at the surface interface with relatively little interaction with the material. The portion of the light that is not specularly reflected penetrates the surface interface, where it interacts with colorant material. This light is absorbed and scattered before making its way back through the interface. Such highly scattered light constitutes the diffuse component.

Most homogenous materials, on the other hand, can be classified into two broad categories based on how they scatter light: metals and nonmetals. Metals are opaque because of their high conductivity. Light cannot penetrate an appreciable distance into the surface of a metal without exciting electrons that absorb and reradiate the energy as light. Therefore, metals do not have a diffuse component, and their reflection is described entirely as specular. In the case of colored metals, the electronic structure of the metal will cause certain wavelengths to be absorbed and converted to heat energy rather than reradiated, so that the spectrum is altered in reflection.

Nonmetals such as glass, transparent plastic, and water, on the other hand, have low conductivity. Having no conducting electrons and typically no other mechanism to absorb visible light, uniform nonmetals are generally transparent. When light falls on the surface of a nonmetal, a portion of the light is reflected and the remainder passes entirely through the material. For this reason, when we look at a pane of glass, we can see a reflection of ourselves as well as light through the glass.

As light passes from one transparent or translucent material to another, its speed, and consequently its direction, is changed. This property of glass is exploited in optical lenses. The best explanation for this bending, or *refraction,* can be found in the famous equations of light and magnetism formulated by the nineteenth-century Scottish physicist James Clerk Maxwell. Every transparent material has an *index of refraction,* derived from Maxwell's equations, that determines, for different angles of incidence, the angle through which light will bend when it passes from a vacuum into the material. Air, for example, has a very low index of refraction, meaning that light scarcely is affected by passing through it, while water, glass, and many familiar transparent solids and liquids have larger indices of refraction, which lead to more pronounced bending of light.

The term *transmittance* describes the tendency of a transparent or translucent object to allow different wavelengths of light to pass through it. Light passes not only through some solids and liquids but also through gaseous phenomena such as fog, mist, and smoke. The contribution of light passing through an object or volume to a viewpoint is a product of its transmittance and the spectral power distribution of the incident illuminant.

Light sources, surface reflectance, and transmittance, therefore, all contribute to the amount of light passing from a point in a scene to a viewpoint. The environment of light, however, has one further subtlety. In the natural world, light will scatter from object to object and its spectral power distribution will change with each colored surface it encounters. The light scattered from a white wall near a blue rug, for example, has a bluish tint because some light scatters from the rug to the wall to the viewpoint. The blue light reflected from the rug effectively acts as another source of illumination.

SPOTLIGHT In this image, the computer is modeling a second light source which is evident in added highlights. The computer simulates the effect of a spotlight by limiting the influence of the illumination to a certain angular extent. Part of the image, particularly the topmost tetrahedron, is outside the cone of the spotlight illumination.

One has only to glance around a room illuminated by a single lamp to observe that indirect reflections are quite significant. It is unlikely that any surface, even those hidden from the lamp, will be totally dark because the ceilings and walls reflect light and scatter illumination. Light arising from such interreflections is commonly referred to as *ambient* illumination and it constitutes an important component of realistic, perceptually satisfying images. In daylight, scattering from the atmosphere provides a high level of ambient illumination.

Illumination Models

If computer graphics images are to appear verisimilar, the computer must be formally instructed to calculate each of these qualities of light. The first step, therefore, is to propose a mathematical model that describes how light behaves, how it is transported to and reflected by different surfaces. In computer graphics, the terms *illumination model*, *shading model*, and *reflection model* are used somewhat interchangeably to describe this mathematical model.

An illumination model describes two properties of light: the manner in which light is radiated from light sources and its behavior when it encounters surfaces, including, in some models, interreflections. The computer uses mathematical equations to simulate the manner in which light is modified by reflection from or transmission through the objects it encounters. The equations include various functions of lighting parameters, such as diffuse reflectance, specular reflectance, surface roughness, transmittance, viewing direction, and illumination direction. To obtain a final approximation of light scattered to the viewer, the computer uses the equations to calculate the contributions from the light sources and any interreflections individually and adds them together. The mathematical equations range from simple, empirically judged models that can be rapidly calculated to extremely sophisticated models incorporating the physics of the interaction of light and matter even including, in some cases, the microscopic geometry of surface roughness.

RENDERING

The four main categories of rendering techniques, the computer scientists' schemata, are *ray casting, polygon rendering* (discussed in Chapter 6, "Beyond Appearances"), *ray tracing,* and *radiosity.*

The first two of these, ray casting and polygon rendering, employ *local illumination models*—that is, they model only the light reflected directly from light sources. They do not model secondary reflection from surface to surface. In this type of rendering, there is always the danger that a surface will not be directly illuminated, resulting in a black area in the image. To prevent this, local illumination models introduce a uniform, pervasive, nondirectional source of light. This type of light source is akin to skylight on a cloudy day, where the illumination is exceedingly flat.

Images generated through ray casting and polygon rendering using local illumination models may not appear realistic because they neglect interreflections. Ray tracing and radiosity, on the other hand, model the path of the illuminant from surface to surface and ultimately to the viewer. These techniques are said to model the illumination globally. In this way, these *global illumination models* create a much more satisfying environment of light in the rendered image.

The choice of the illumination model will produce cues that are perceived as different qualities of the environment of light. Early computer graphics images, for example, have a synthetic quality, resulting from the

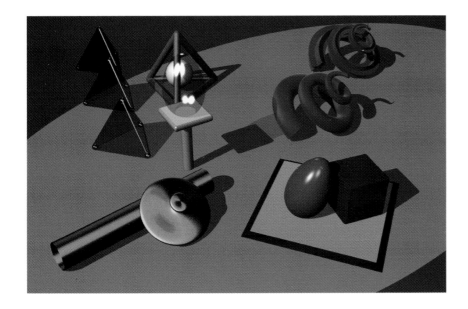

SHADOWS In the earlier image, the spotlight did not cast shadows. The addition of the shadows in this image demonstrates that the computer must be specifically instructed to model every aspect of illumination, and that illumination models need not obey the laws of physics.

use of a particular local illumination model. Surfaces often appear as if they are made of plastic because this model assumes surfaces are geometrically smooth and have sharp highlights that are the color of the light source. At the time these computer graphics images were made, computers were not powerful enough to model and render surfaces with richer reflectance properties. By contrast, ray tracing often produces images with sharp reflections and crisp shadows. This crystalline appearance results from following only the rays that would be reflected from a perfectly mirrored surface. In the natural world, however, light reflects in many directions. Radiosity treats interreflections from area to area rather than from point to point. This treatment produces a softer and more diffuse environment of light, yet one that may lack highlights and glossy surfaces.

Ray Tracing

Ray tracing generates some of the most realistic computer-generated images, so realistic that they are sometimes indistinguishable from photographs. To achieve this level of verisimilitude, ray tracing follows each reflection and refraction of light. This is not simple, but there are some shortcuts. Among the large number of rays emanating from the light

PENUMBRAE In the real world, shadows often have soft edges because light sources radiate from more than a single point. In this image, such an area light source has been simulated. Shadows are now softer. The shadow from the table, for example, now varies continuously from light to dark, a transition known as a penumbra.

sources in a scene, only those that reach the viewpoint, either directly or through reflection, need be considered. The vast majority of light rays are inconsequential because they never reach the image plane. Ray tracing and ray casting, therefore, make an intractable problem more manageable by following rays from the viewpoint through each pixel into the scene and ultimately to the light sources.

Starting from the viewpoint and passing through a single pixel in the image plane, a ray will eventually encounter either a surface or a light source. If it is a surface, the question arises as to whether that surface point is illuminated. This question can be answered by attempting to draw a straight line between the surface point and all of the points in the scene that are defined as light sources. These lines are called *shadow rays* because they determine whether or not the surface point is in shadow. If an uninterrupted line can be drawn from the surface point to a light source, then the point is not in shadow. If, on the other hand, the shadow ray intersects another surface on its way to the light source, the surface point will be in shadow with respect to that light source.

For each light source that is not shadowed, the computer utilizes a reflection model, as noted earlier, to determine the light from that light source that is scattered to the viewpoint. This color contribution is, along with all other light source contributions, added to the pixel color.

GLOBAL ILLUMINATION The human visual system is extremely sensitive to subtle qualities of illumination that can be simulated by lighting models that include interreflections. Such lighting models are called *global* and are distinguished from lighting models that simulate only local interactions of light and surface. In this image, highly specular surfaces such as the glossy tile and the egg (lower right) can be seen to reflect their environment, and light refracts through transparent objects such as the egg on the table and the tetrahedra.

Computer graphics would be a far simpler discipline if we could stop right here, and, in fact, that is what we do with ray casting and other techniques that use local illumination models. Modeling interreflections, although it requires the additional hard work of ray tracing or other global illumination models, is worthwhile, however, because we can satisfy our perceptual hunger for verisimilitude.

Computer scientists have developed various ray-tracing algorithms to model light from interreflections. In its original form, ray tracing assumes that the initial ray from the viewpoint into the scene may be a mirrorlike reflection. Euclid, in fact, established the principle that when light reflects from a perfectly smooth surface, "the angle of incidence equals the angle of reflection." When a light ray encounters a surface, the angle between the surface and the direction of approach of the ray will be equal to the angle between the surface and the reflected ray. Ray tracing, in this case, follows the presumed incident ray to determine whether it encounters any surfaces. If it does encounter a surface, that surface, if illuminated, will function as a light source and will illuminate the original surface point that defines the color of the pixel.

Of course the contribution of the second surface point will depend upon the interaction of all of the illuminants and its own surface reflectance. The second surface point therefore must be treated exactly as the first surface point in the sense that shadow rays and incident rays will define the illumination affecting its apparent color. The incident ray from the second surface point may encounter a third surface that will need to be treated as a third surface point that is influencing the second and the first. In this sense, ray tracing is recursive: each successive surface point becomes a viewpoint in relation to the subsequent surface point.

Our ray-traced world is almost complete. If we were to calculate images at this point, however, windows would be opaque, water would appear as mercury, and a cup of tea might resemble wood. The procedures we have described so far do not account for the fact that some materials are transparent or translucent. To model these properties of objects, ray tracing generally assumes that the initial ray from the viewpoint may also be *refracted*. The index of refraction is used to compute the deflection of a light ray both as it enters the transparent material and as it exits the other side. This refracted ray then is recursively traced into the environment in the same manner as reflected rays.

Ray tracing simulates reflection and refraction with great accuracy and, as a result, produces highly realistic images. For example, if a scene contains a magnifying glass, the index of refraction and curvature of the lens can be specified to the computer. The ray tracing calculations will then render objects seen through the glass as magnified. Even rainbows and mirages can be reproduced by modeling the refraction of the water droplets or heated air that give rise to these phenomena in nature.

Ray tracing, in its original form, assumes the specular reflection, the mirrorlike property of surfaces, to be extremely important and, in fact, follows only the mirrorlike reflections from surface to surface. Ray tracing thus treats diffuse reflection locally; it does not attempt to model diffuse interreflection. The computational demands of modeling all of the interreflecting diffuse rays can be excessive; however computer scientists have extended ray tracing to model these diffuse rays. Instead of recursively tracing only one or two light rays from a surface point into its environment, some models follow hundreds or thousands of rays of light. Sophisticated algorithms have been developed to track only those light rays that contribute significantly to pixel color. These techniques result in images with an even more faithful reproduction of the environment of light.

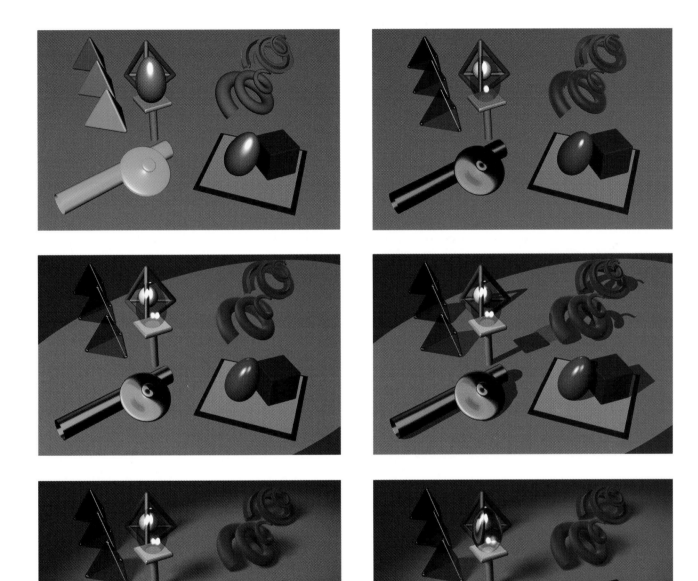

SIMULATING LIGHT Direct comparison of the final six images in the series illustrates the high degree of control that the algorithm designer has over properties of light in the computer. Of course, there is no actual separable light and surface in these rendered images; they are simply patterns of colors on the printed page. Nonetheless, each rendering algorithm, each image, will trigger your visual system to synthesize complementary illumination and surface worlds.

Radiosity

For many years computer scientists struggled to come to terms with the diffuse quality of natural light. As noted earlier, interreflections guarantee there are rarely any completely dark areas in a room even if there is only one light. Radiosity is the computer scientist's preliminary effort to create a warm and diffuse illumination environment.

It is perhaps fitting that the concepts used to "warm up" computer graphics renderings are, in fact, derived from thermal engineering. Radiosity is based upon techniques traditionally used to solve energy balance problems. In furnace design, for example, an engineer typically needs to determine how energy will flow among components. The rate at which heat leaves a surface, the flow of energy per unit time, is equal to the rate at which that surface radiates heat plus the rate at which it reflects heat from other surfaces. In the normal course of events, equilibrium is reached when, for any two surfaces, the amount of energy flowing in one direction is equal to that flowing in the other. Indeed, if they are not equal, then the surface transferring more heat will lose energy to the other surface until the rate of transfer equalizes.

In radiosity, light is modeled in the same manner. All of the surfaces in the scene are divided into regular patches, each of which is considered to be both an emitter and reflector of light energy. The rate at which each patch radiates light is assumed to be equal to the rate of emission plus the rate of reflection from all other patches. Like ray tracing, radiosity is recursive. The model may begin with the light sources and transfer light energy to all of the surfaces in the scene. Each of the surfaces is then treated as a light source that radiates to all of the other surfaces in the scene, and the process continues, eventually reaching an equilibrium, or steady state.

A critical aspect of a radiosity computation is the manner in which the surfaces are broken into discrete patches. An entire wall, a desktop, or a floor could be regarded as a single patch that emits and reflects light. Although the rendering computation would be tremendously simplified by such an assumption, it would not produce a satisfactory visual result. For example, a desk lamp will cast more light on areas near the lamp than on regions of the desktop that are farther away. If the desktop is treated as a single patch, however, it will be rendered with a single value for its light energy. To achieve a more realistic appearance, it is necessary to break the

RADIOSITY In the natural world, the reflection of light from surface to surface creates a subtle illumination environment that is difficult to model with a computer. One technique for modeling interreflections is radiosity. Radiosity simplifies the computation by assuming that all surfaces are diffuse reflectors. In this synthetic radiosity image, the sunlit patch of bricks illuminates the walls and ceilings of this courtyard with a reddish light. Note that if the computer had omitted interreflections, most of this scene would be black.

surfaces up into patches that are sufficiently small so that light does not appear to attenuate in perceptible steps. Similarly, if a patch spans a shadow boundary, there will be no distinct boundary because the patch cannot be both in and out of the shadow simultaneously. Patches often are created such that their edges coincide with shadow edges to avoid this problem.

The original radiosity methods assume that all the surfaces in a scene are Lambertian diffuse reflectors and, consequently, that the intensity of light reflected from a surface is independent of the viewing direction. This assumption significantly simplifies the mathematical equations. Additionally, the Lambertian assumption eliminates the requirement of knowing the viewpoint when calculating the shading. In essence, a shaded environment is computed only once and can be rendered from any viewpoint. Since shading is not recalculated as the viewpoint changes, the display computation is fast, and radiosity solutions can be viewed interactively.

LIGHT AND VISUAL COMPUTING

It is tempting to think that the computer graphics modeler can bypass all of the problems of surface color that afflict the painter interested in naturalism. In mixing colors, a painter is deciding simultaneously how to capture all illumination and surface reflectance contributions. This is no small feat, and the schema the artist uses will create a characteristic treatment of the environment of light. An inspection of a painting by John Constable or Rembrandt demonstrates that the pigments used to represent objects are hardly the actual surface colors. Constable used dozens of colors to depict, for example, the leaves on a tree, which technically speaking are all the same color before they interact with light in the scene.

Unfortunately the computer scientist is rarely able to "model the physics." The process is just too complicated. Every light source with its particular spectral power distribution and shape, every surface with its particular orientation, roughness, and surface reflectance, and all interreflections would need to be modeled. The computational demands of modeling these properties of light and surface usually preclude this approach, particularly when images need to be generated quickly for an animated sequence or for real-time interaction. As a result, approximations are made that tend to leave one or another stylistic imprint on the rendered image. Thus, computer graphics modelers and artists share a similar dilemma, the need to choose among schemata, each with strengths and limitations for simulating particular qualities of light.

An Infinity of Pyramids
4

The body of the air is full of an infinite number of radiant pyramids caused by the objects located in it. These pyramids intersect and interweave without interfering with each other during their independent passage throughout the air in which they are infused. They are of equal power, and all can be equal to each and each equal to all. The semblance of a body is carried by them as a whole into all parts of the air, and each smallest part receives into itself the image that has been caused.

— *Leonardo*

ONE FROM MANY This photomosaic of the Trapezium, a star cluster located within the Orion Nebula, was assembled from several photographs taken with the Hubble Space Telescope. The resulting image has a wider field of view and a higher resolution than any single Hubble photograph. In light field rendering, images are treated as records of light and are mathematically combined in three dimensions. By pooling information from multiple images, the entire three-dimensional environment of light is encoded within the computer, and images from new, inferred perspectives can be constructed. Light field rendering adds the encoding and processing of light fields to computer graphics. The computer containing a light field is a kind of infinitely versatile camera that captures all images from all points of view.

The techniques of geometric modeling, ray casting, and ray tracing would have delighted Leonardo. Indeed, the whole methodology of computer graphics described in the previous chapter—forming geometric descriptions and imitating the straight paths of light from the view point to light sources—would have been familiar to all of the inventors of perspective.

To Leonardo, the concept of the visual pyramid raised some interesting questions about the nature of light. After all, wherever the eye rests, wherever the artist sets up a *camera obscura*, an image will be formed.

Leonardo recognized that, since any point constitutes a viewpoint, there is an infinite number of contemporaneous visual pyramids, each with its light rays passing through the others. A description of the scene carried by this field of light must be represented in some manner at every point.

Fields of light have the well-known and intriguing property of a hologram in that, in a sense, each part represents the whole. A hologram can be cut into many small pieces with a scissors and each piece will project a replica of the entire scene. What if one could use a computer to capture the information at every point in a field of light as a hologram does? The task would require processing a massive, perhaps prohibitive, quantity of information, but the computer is suited to just such data-intensive tasks. One can only speculate what kind of pleasure Leonardo might have taken in this use of a digital computer, a machine now adapted to exploring his idea of an infinity of pyramids.

Such an approach to visual computing is a far cry from modeling geometry and light as described in the previous chapter. In that mode, objects are formed in darkness first and then secondarily illuminated with one or another variety of modeled light. Indeed, the earliest visual computing experiments produced mere wireframes with no illumination at all. *Light field rendering,* the subject of this chapter, by contrast, forgoes objects altogether. Light, at long last, is not an afterthought, not something overlaid on a dark, geometric universe, but the first and only consideration in this form of computer graphics.

IMAGE MOSAICS

Light field rendering has its origins in the early days of image processing, although scientists at the time did not foresee that the techniques they were developing would take this direction. In the 1950s, image processing pioneers at NASA's Jet Propulsion Laboratory (JPL) in Pasadena, California, laboring in a new field with unknown technical demands,

LUNAR MAPPING In 1994, the Clementine spacecraft captured nearly 2 million close-up images of the lunar surface. This composite of some of these images reproduces the Moon as it would appear from Earth. Each of the constituent images is a transection of its own visual pyramid, which does not correspond to the visual pyramid defining the composite. To produce this image, therefore, the smaller images were warped digitally and brought into alignment with the new visual pyramid.

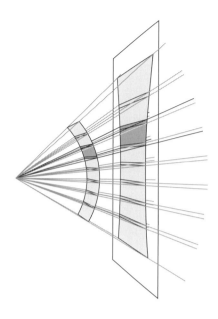

PYRAMIDS WITH SHARED RAYS The eight images of the Pulgas Water Temple shown here were photographed with a camera mounted on a tripod. As is illustrated in the schematic above, the camera was pointed in several directions to capture different viewing pyramids. One viewing pyramid is depicted by black lines. The unprocessed images will not fit together to form a proper mosaic because their image planes are not aligned. To make the composite on the far right, a perspective distortion was applied to transform each image from its own image plane to the composite image plane. The composite image plane has a wider field of view than any of the constituent images. This technique is possible because the larger, composite viewing pyramid and the eight original viewing pyramids share the same rays of light.

developed the first digital imaging techniques for processing lunar and planetary imagery.

These image processing algorithms were designed to solve relatively simple problems. Computers were used, for example, to remove defects from digitized television images returned from the Ranger spacecraft on their missions to the moon. Computer scientists working with space imagery became more and more ambitious, and within a decade digital image processing became an important tool for space exploration and began to be applied in many other fields.

Mapping was an important goal for early lunar exploration. With an eye on moon landings, the National Aeronautics and Space Administration (NASA) needed extremely detailed images of the lunar surface. Unfortunately, early electronic cameras could only capture and process a limited amount of information, with a field of view fixed to a small angle and thus to a small area of the moon. To create larger fields of view, JPL scientists devised a way to stitch together thousands of photographs sent back by Ranger and other orbiters into larger images, *photomosaics,* which could be used as maps for later moon landings.

The process of creating such a photomosaic begins with thousands of visual pyramids, each captured from a different location as a spacecraft surveys the moon. The various pyramids, none of which share the same image plane, must be composited into a single image with one larger, inferred visual pyramid, which represents the whole visible surface. To simulate how the moon would look when photographed in a single picture plane, with only one visual pyramid, the JPL scientists developed algorithms for translating, rotating, and warping the individual images to form a composite.

The figure on the facing page demonstrates how images from different visual pyramids need to be processed in order to construct a single image with a wider field of view. Visual computing researcher Paul Haeberli photographed eight sections of the Pulgas Water Temple, a structure built in 1938 to celebrate the completion of the Hetch Hetchy Aqueduct in Northern California. The camera was placed on a tripod and rotated a few degrees between each exposure, so that the viewpoint remained constant while the image plane was changed.

When the images are simply composited without being transformed, they do not match. Notice that the temple columns in adjacent images do not meet and the lines forming the steps are broken. The reason for

this is that each image is a cross section of a visual pyramid originating from the position of the camera for that image. The value of a pixel in this image is the brightness of the light from the scene passing through that pixel to the location of the camera. The complete photomosaic is, itself, a transection of a still larger viewing pyramid. The problem is that each smaller image does not share the same image plane. Rather, their visual pyramids are tilted with respect both to one another and to the final, larger visual pyramid.

These images can be united into a photomosaic because the composite shares the same light rays as the smaller photographs, even though the smaller images and the photomosaic have different image planes. The value of a pixel in the photomosaic can be determined by tracing the light ray that passes from the camera position through the pixel and into the scene. This ray is identical to a ray in one of the smaller images that starts at the camera, passes through one of its pixels, and continues into the scene. The value of the pixel in the photomosaic is the same as the value of the pixel in the smaller image because they encode precisely the same light from the temple.

When the light from all of the pixels of a single, smaller image is composited into the photomosaic, what was once a rectangular image becomes trapezoidal. This warping of the smaller image is known as a *projective* transformation. When the original photographs overlap, some pixels encode identical light rays. This redundancy was used by Haeberli to determine, with the computer, the best projective transformations to align all of the images. The shared rays were blended together in the final image.

MARTIAN PANORAMA An image is the record of all light that passes through a two-dimensional surface at a given moment in time. The surface need not be flat, however. The Mars Pathfinder, an unmanned probe that landed on the Martian surface in the summer of 1997, was equipped with a pair of cameras located atop a vertical riser with a rotating base. It could capture images of the landscape in any direction, each with 256 pixels on a side. Individual images, captured and transmitted one by one back to Earth, were stitched together into panoramic images of much higher resolution, showing the sweeping Martian landscape. To make the panorama shown above, JPL scientists used the computer to calculate the way the environment of light would project onto a cylinder surrounding the spacecraft. The image is essentially the flattened cylinder. The first panoramic images had block artifacts, as the constituent images, each with its own flat image plane, were simply tiled together, one on top of the other. Computer scientists used more sophisticated stitching algorithms to warp and blend the images into this cylindrical projection.

Similar techniques were employed by the JPL scientists to create their photomosaics of the moon, and they are a fundamental technique used in planetary imaging. After the Mariner mission to Mars in 1971, for instance, a compositing technique was used to produce a Martian globe 4 feet in diameter from thousands of individual images. Photomosaic maps have also been made of the outer planets and their moons and are used to create images of regions of the universe too big to be photographed in a single image, such as large areas viewed from the Hubble Space Telescope.

Panoramic Images

A particularly useful type of photomosaic is constructed from a cylindrical series of images. The series can be obtained by rotating a tripod-mounted camera 360 degrees, capturing a photograph every few

A VIEW OF DELFT The idea of a curved projection is not new. It has been conjectured that this painting by Carel Fabritius, a seventeenth-century Dutch painter renowned for his interest in perspective, was designed to be bent into a hemicylinder in the back of a box and viewed through a small hole. When viewed this way, the image appears, more or less, in proper linear perspective. The physical bending and viewing of Fabritius's painting is analogous to the computational warping that permits us to create images in proper linear perspective from a panoramic image.

degrees. The procedure for creating a cylindrical panorama is different from that Haeberli used to make a photomosaic because the individual images are projected to a cylinder instead of a flat picture plane. The entire cylindrical image can be unrolled and printed flat as a rectangle, but the image will be distorted. Straight lines will appear curved in the flattened image. Undistorted images, however, can be produced from the panorama by reprojecting the cylindrical image onto a flat plane.

The unique property of a panoramic image, given that the camera is rotated 360 degrees, is that the panorama records light passing through a particular viewpoint from all directions. Since all the light has been sampled, any visual pyramid with that viewpoint can be reconstructed by the computer—even pyramids that were not captured photographically. The cylinder is a unique record from which many images can be extracted. In short, if we can imagine repeating this panoramic view at many points, we are one step closer to the ideal of light field rendering, to encoding *all* light in the scene.

ENVIRONMENT MAPPING The visual computer is leading to a new definition of an image. The traditional view that an image is a pattern of light captured in a plane is giving way to the notion of capturing a field of light at a given instant in time that may have any shape. In this illustration, Paul Debevec has captured a spherical light field with high dynamic range, which is then used to model reflections and refractions in a computer graphics scene. The light field was obtained by photographing a small, mirrored sphere and then projecting the image, in the computer, onto a large cube surrounding these objects. The image was rendered with standard ray tracing techniques, with the illumination directly represented in the cube image. A ray is projected from the viewpoint into the scene where it reflects from surface to surface until,

perhaps, it reflects to the interior surface of the surrounding cube. The pixel color is determined both by the surface properties of the objects and the light field value represented at this intersection on the cube.

This representation of the light surrounding a point in a scene is known as an *environment map.* Environment mapping, in a more simplified fashion than in this example, is commonly used to add realism to highly reflective surfaces. An environment map need not be a cube. A cylindrical, panoramic image is, in fact, another representation of an environment map. Since an environment map is a portion of a light field, environment mapping is an example of the convergence of geometry-based computer graphics and light field rendering.

GEOMETRY IN FIELDS OF LIGHT This computer-generated image of the Matterhorn blurs the distinction between modeling geometry and light field rendering. The image was made with a rough geometric model of this 15,000-foot peak in Switzerland's Pennine Alps. Instead of attempting the formidable task of constructing an accurate model of the geometry of the mountain and lighting it, an aerial photograph was projected onto this simplified model to create the illusion of light and detail. This process, called *texture mapping,* applies a two-dimensional array of pixels onto a three-dimensional model. There is no light and surface modeling in this image. All shading is encoded in the projected photograph. This texture map, therefore, is appropriate only for a single lighting environment. Other images can be used for reproducing different illumination conditions. Texture mapping and environment mapping are two examples of the many ways in which captured light is used in visual computing. (Geospecific data courtesy of Remote Sensing Laboratories, University of Zurich and the Swiss Federal Office of Topography.)

LIGHT FIELD RENDERING

In creating both photomosaics and panoramic computer images, the computer scientist has given up geometry-based visual computing for something quite different. Recreating the world of objects in the computer with our techniques for describing geometries, and illuminating them, has its appeal. In geometry-based computer graphics, we are creating an alternate universe where, however impoverished it may seem when compared to the real universe, we have complete authority. Even the laws of physics, inviolable throughout the rest of the universe, are options that may be enabled or disabled in the world of simulated objects and light. It is a powerful opportunity, but it also has its limitations. Modeling is difficult and, as we have seen in earlier chapters, the devil is in the details. Recreating the complexity and nuance of the natural world is an enormous challenge. We have an appetite for realism that is often difficult to satisfy.

In light field rendering, on the other hand, the data processed by the computer describe not three-dimensional objects but fields of light. The computer scientist is exploiting Leonardo's idea of the coexistence of an infinite number of overlapping visual pyramids. It is tempting to think of light fields simply as arrays of numbers, where a number represents the light passing through a given point traveling in a particular direction. An image can be seen as a portion of that array, a bundle of rays that pass through the same point, the viewpoint, and through the image pixels. The good news is that it is possible to join images together, even though they have different viewpoints, because in aggregate they encode rays of light from which a new, virtual viewpoint can be inferred. Extending this logic, the computer can be used to travel through a visual universe, generating synthetic viewpoints along the way, made from any number of individual images that are different perspectives of the same objects. Such a universe, achieved with visual computing, would have the appearance of the natural world in all its complexity and subtlety because it is constituted of real-world light fields.

The figure on page 68, illustrating the work of Marc Levoy and Pat Hanrahan of Stanford University, is an example of how the computer can be used to process full fields of light. In this case, the scene, a Buddha figure, has been computer-generated with the traditional geometric techniques described in previous chapters. But that is incidental, because Levoy and Hanrahan, from this point forward, use only light field techniques to generate images.

As with both previously described photomosaics and panoramic images, many images are made of the same scene from different viewpoints. Conceptually, Levoy's and Hanrahan's technique has three elements: the Buddha, a focal plane that can be thought of as a window through which the Buddha can be seen, and a camera plane where a collection of initial viewpoints is located. A sample of twenty-five of the images that have been made at twenty-five points in the camera plane are shown to differ slightly, one from the other, in perspective, a consequence of the fact that each point in the camera plane acts as its own viewing point. It is as if a collection of twenty-five cameras were dispersed in the same plane and used to capture all of the images simultaneously.

There is sufficient information in this collection of different perspectives to reconstruct intermediate perspectives from other viewpoints in the camera plane. It is also possible to reconstruct viewpoints either behind or in front of the camera plane. To calculate a perspective from a point behind the camera plane, for example, a visual pyramid is extended

through the camera and focal planes. Every pixel in this computed image can be associated with a line drawn from the viewpoint, through the new image plane, through the camera plane, and through the focal plane. This ray is uniquely identified by the coordinates on the camera and focal planes through which it passes. These four coordinates, the horizontal and vertical locations from each plane, determine a unique location in a four-dimensional lookup table. To calculate an image with a viewpoint in front of the camera plane, a similar technique is used, the only difference being that the viewing rays are extended *behind* the viewpoint to the camera plane in order to specify a location in the four-dimensional lookup table.

This lookup table is a unique representation of the scene. It has been populated with values from the original set of images, and it represents a field of light from which images can be calculated that were not specifically recorded. Values for some images will need to be interpolated because the pixel positions for the new synthesized images will not always perfectly match cells in the four-dimensional lookup table. But the more images that are used to build up the lookup table, the less interpolation will need to be done, and the sharper the final images will be. Furthermore, the images that are used to build up the lookup table do not need to be coplanar. If we record images above, below, and behind a scene, it is possible to reconstruct any visual pyramid.

With light field rendering the computer seems to be storing every possible image in every possible direction from every possible viewpoint—the entire infinity of pyramids spoken of by Leonardo is held together as a field of light. To create an image we need only reference, and possibly interpolate, the values in a lookup table determined by a given viewpoint and viewing direction.

Some of the well-known properties of holograms have their equivalent in the multidimensional lookup table created with the light field rendering technique. If a hologram is cut in half, for example, the entire scene can still be reconstructed, but the field of view will be restricted. The equivalent in light field rendering would be to cut the camera or focal plane in half. In either case, the field of view will be restricted, although the remaining viewpoints would still reconstruct the entire scene. When either the camera or focal plane is reduced, there are fewer viewing pyramids that intersect both planes and thus index valid locations in the four-dimensional table.

All forms of imaging are attempts to capture a particular visual experience. Both holography and light field rendering are methods for

AN INFINITY OF PYRAMIDS Sometimes in image making it is tempting to think of the environment as a sea of light that may be sampled, in one way or another, to produce an image. The simplest case is to snap a picture with a camera, which has one viewing pyramid and one projection to an image plane. The resulting image represents the light in the scene as it would appear from only one viewpoint and viewing direction. Marc Levoy and Pat Hanrahan of Stanford University have explored a more versatile means of sampling the light field. In this example, entirely simulated in the computer, they sample a potentially unlimited number of viewing pyramids with coplanar viewpoints, some of which are shown on the facing page. With this data alone, they are able to create images with a wide range of viewing pyramids. One example is given above. The inferred viewpoints can be in front of or behind the camera plane, and the viewing direction can be tilted with respect to the original visual pyramids. It is as if the light field representation encodes all possible viewing pyramids simultaneously. This method of capturing multiple viewing pyramids and reconstructing images from new viewpoints has some kinship with holography.

SOLID SIGHT In stereo photography, a pair of horizontally adjacent exposures are made that correspond to the viewing pyramids of the left and right eyes. A stereoscope can be used to project the left image to the left eye and the right image to the right eye. Depth is perceived because the eye and brain are able to detect disparity between the two perspectives by means of a visual subsense called *stereopsis* (Greek meaning "solid sight"). Objects with great horizontal disparity are perceived to be closer than objects with less disparity.

Three-dimensional computer models can be used to render similarly disparate images that can be perceived stereoscopically. Generating stereo pairs is straightforward. Two images are rendered from horizontally separated viewpoints. The degree of separation and the angulation of the perspectives will determine the apparent size and placement of objects relative to the apparent image plane when the images are fused perceptually. Stereoscopic imaging demonstrates forcefully that the eye and brain are not passive receivers of information but actively organize an internal perceptual world from the light patterns reaching the retinas. The images are two-dimensional, yet they give rise to a three-dimensional visual world that, in fact, exists only in the perceiver.

encoding, not just a single visual pyramid, but a light field from which new visual pyramids can be derived. Both techniques suggest the possibility of an interactive, synthetic visual environment that would be indistinguishable from reality and, thus, would fulfill a latent aspiration of technologists since the beginning of imaging.

A PERFECT CAMERA

Light field rendering connects computer graphics with the classical concept of the visual pyramid in a new way. Previously, in the case of geometric modeling, the visual pyramid was used to describe the relationship between a viewpoint and points in the scene: the visual pyramid defined the rays of light that required modeling. In the case of light field rendering, there are no geometric models, only fields of light and viewpoints. It is a method, not of recreating physical objects, but of recording information about the environment of light, a kind of perfect camera that captures not one but all visual pyramids.

Leonardo's vision of "an infinity of pyramids" conjures a universe filled not only with an incalculable number of alternative viewpoints but also with an infinite number of light rays intersecting at each point. Any point contains the information necessary to reconstruct any visual pyramid from that point, a possibility that depends upon a curious property of electromagnetic waves: they leave no residual effect as they pass through one another.

Such a picture, a conflagration of intersecting light rays, is the input data for human vision. In contrast with this unseen turmoil, our visual world is striking for its stability and order. This transformation of inchoate light into an intricate and equable visual world results from the extraordinary organizing power of vision. This organizing power, this hunger for detail and nuance, is a fundamental imperative driving the advancement of visual computing.

A Sorcerer's Apprentice
5

The screen is a window through which one looks into a virtual world. The challenge is to make the world look real, sound real, feel real, and interact realistically.
—*Ivan Sutherland, 1965*

PROCEDURAL GRAPHICS Real-world practitioners of computer graphics rely upon higher-level interfaces to automate image synthesis. These *procedural graphics* techniques are used to direct the activity of the computer as it builds a complex three-dimensional model or as it shades an image. Here, an imitation of one of Claude Monet's haystack paintings has been rendered from a three-dimensional model. The orientation and position of simulated brush strokes have been determined procedurally by the computer, based upon the three-dimensional geometry of the haystacks. A procedural shading model was used to determine pixels in each stroke that imitate a painterly treatment of light.

If it were possible to play the history of visual computing in fast motion, it would look like a new universe being born, an imperfect mirror of our own. At first, light in the computer illuminates only a dead and angular universe. Soon, however, there are stirrings. Where once there were only simple objects made from thinly disguised primitives, there are now cascades, rain, clouds, fire and smoke, broad landscapes, and mountains ranging toward the horizon. Later, there are organic forms, plants, grassy savannas, and trees with leaves rustling in the wind. Finally, there are animals in our alternate computer universe, flocks of flying birds and schools of swimming fish, not merely lock-step robots, but seemingly independent creatures that scatter, recombine, and interact in playful ways, as if in nature.

As we shall see in this chapter, computer scientists have directed the unbounded zeal of the computer for executing instructions, no matter how repetitive or arduous, to give the computer graphics universe a whole new kind of energy and diversity.

One of the greatest challenges of computer graphics is modeling geometrically intricate objects and simulating their environment of light. Constructing three-dimensional objects such as plants, animals, rock formations, and landscapes by hand from cones, cylinders, spheres, and polygons is far too difficult, as is explicitly specifying the illumination and surface shading in the subtlest detail.

A variety of techniques, known collectively as *procedural graphics,* have been developed, however, whereby the computer does most of the work. The tableau of a computer scientist creating a procedure that executes instructions is evocative of Goethe's poem, *The Sorcerer's Apprentice.* As the story goes, when a sorcerer leaves his apprentice in charge of the workshop, the lazy apprentice casts a spell so that a broom will draw a bucket of water. The broom follows the instructions literally and relentlessly draws bucket after bucket. When the broom is chopped in half, in an effort to stop it, both halves start drawing water. In Goethe's story the apprentice's attempt to have the broom do his bidding leads to turmoil. In procedural graphics, the ability of the computer to tirelessly execute repetitive instructions has a happier ending.

PARTICLE-BASED SYSTEMS

Many phenomena found in nature can be modeled by breaking them down into separate, interacting elements. Imagine, for example, the movement of a small sphere, perhaps the size of a marble, with the same density as water, so that it neither sinks nor floats as it flows down a river and over a waterfall. That sphere, or *particle,* weaves and bobs in many different directions, up and down and from side to side in eddies and vortices, even as its overall trajectory follows the general flow of the water. If we add additional particles, we observe that there is some regularity to

PARTICLE CASCADE It would be impractical or impossible to model a waterfall by individually designating geometric primitives. Here, a particle system is used to simulate the flow of water. The computer determines the starting positions and the velocities of particles at the top of the waterfall and traces their irregular paths all the way to the bottom. Once the particles have been generated, they are assigned colors, and an image of the scene can be rendered. The particle system incorporates some of the physical properties of water as well as the effect of gravity and the geometry of the rocks. The combined influence of these variables leads to the scattering of particles evident as the mist at the bottom of the cascade.

their movement. If we could characterize with mathematics the nature of the typical movement of such particles, we could begin to model what happens when they are brought together in large numbers.

To model a waterfall, the computer is used to generate tens of thousands of individual particles that will behave, generally speaking, like water when flowing over a ledge and dropping down to the ground. Each particle has a position, shape, and color that will determine pixel values when we render an image that represents a single instant in time. The particles have specific velocities and lifetimes so that additional images can be generated that represent successive moments and can together form an animated sequence that depicts the cascading water dynamically.

The particle systems approach has been used effectively to model not only water but also a large variety of dynamic processes, including fireworks, smoke, and fire. Of course, the particles used to imitate these other phenomena are programmed to behave in a manner that is completely different from the particles designed to simulate the flow of water. The particle modeling approach can also be used to generate static but intricate structures. For example, particles can be designed to generate thousands of blades of grass to form a meadow or trees to form a forest, where each blade of grass or branch of the tree is treated as a single particle. Here the particles trace out a path that, it is hoped, models the shape of the blades or branches so that the human designer does not need to.

Behavioral Modeling

A qualitatively different kind of procedural graphics is *behavioral modeling*. Behavioral modeling introduces into computer simulation the idea that the modeled entity must be able to, in some sense, perceive. Consider, for example, the challenge of modeling a flock of birds. A real flock of birds behaves in an *emergent* manner—the birds have characteristic patterns of interaction as a group. This can only be successfully modeled by a system in which the individuals are influenced by their surroundings. The flocking of birds can be simulated with a modified particle system. Instead of depicting the particles themselves in the final image, as is done with a waterfall, the particles each represent a single bird in a larger set. When the

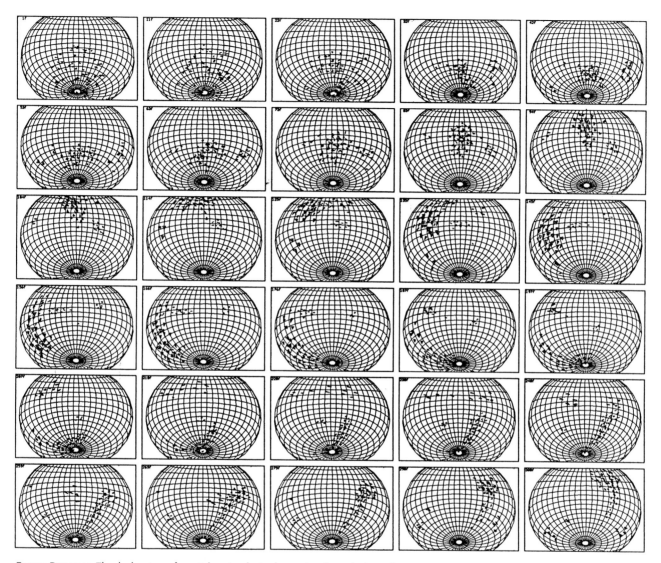

FLYING PARTICLES The behavior of social animals is determined partly by others in a group. The flocking of birds is an example of such emergent behavior and is here modeled with a particle system where the behavior of each member is determined by the position and velocity of the other birds. In this sequence of images, each bird is represented as a triangle, and the flocking pattern within the sphere can be followed left to right, top to bottom. This complex, automatically generated flocking behavior demonstrates the value of the computer as a creative partner. Procedural techniques, such as this example of behavioral modeling, are helping us to understand the richness and complexity of the physical and biological world.

MAKING A CLOUD The computer graphics modeler can take advantage of the fact that some objects have small-scale features that are similar to their overall shapes. When this is the case, the entire object can be constructed by reiterating a single description of its geometric qualities at different scales. The first image in this series shows a coarse shape of a cloud generated by a gradually varying random pattern. In each of the subsequent images, a similar random pattern is applied at a smaller scale to add finer detail.

final scene is rendered, the particles are replaced by full geometric descriptions of birds.

Particle systems and behavioral modeling are techniques of visual computing that go beyond the imperative of image making and address the underlying dynamics of nature. To generate waterfalls that have a realistic appearance, flames that dance from a burning log, trees that branch naturally, or flocking birds, models must account for the physical and developmental forces and situational dynamics that give rise to real-world phenomena.

Procedural systems have attracted the interest of a wide range of scientists who are interested in using the computer to study natural processes. For example, astrophysicists have used particle systems to model the collision of galaxies. Developmental biologists have used particle systems to study emergent properties of growth and differentiation. In emergent systems, large-scale phenomena are determined by the interaction of large numbers of independently acting elements. There are many such emergent phenomena in nature: insect colonies, clusters of neurons, and even human social organizations; particle system simulations offer opportunities to gain insight into all of them.

FRACTAL MODELING

Many objects in nature have small details that appear geometrically similar to their larger features. For example, a short section of rugged coastline appears to have the same jaggedness as a longer length. Likewise, a small portion of a cloud often appears to have the same geometric quality as the entire cloud. The geometrically *self-similar* aspect of some objects provides a means for using procedural techniques to generate fine detail from an initially simple description.

The term *fractal,* coined by Benoit Mandelbrot and somewhat loosely applied in computer graphics, describes this quality of self-similarity, in which objects display the same geometric properties irrespective of scale. Fractal geometry is an important area of mathematics that addresses the quality of self-similarity in any phenomenon. In computer graphics, fractal geometry is specifically a means by which a general geometric form is repeatedly scaled down and placed within the original form to create a desired fineness of detail.

For example, to generate a mountain range automatically, we can start with a description of a single rectangle and a rule for modifying it. The rule may be to pick first a midpoint of the rectangle, and then to raise that midpoint off the surface of the rectangle by a random amount to form four four-sided polygons. The computer can reapply the rule to each of the four new polygons. This iterative process can be repeated any number of times until the structure has the desired amount of detail.

GRAMMAR-BASED MODELING

Grammar-based modeling is an approach that has been primarily applied to modeling plants. It is related to fractal geometry, in the sense that successive generations of a model are computed by applying a set of rules iteratively. Grammar-based modeling, however, has greater flexibility in the types of rules that may be utilized.

The term *grammar-based modeling* describes the building of complex structures using rules that have some kinship with the grammatical rules that unite words in language. In language, words are not strung together arbitrarily to convey meaning—there are principles regulating the way in which nouns, verbs, pronouns, and other parts of speech can be combined. Similarly, in grammar-based modeling, rules direct the construction of a particular type of form.

A snowflake pattern known to mathematicians as a Koch curve is a simple example, used by Heinz-Otto Peitgen, Deitmar Saupe, and Harmut Jürgens, to show how grammar-based modeling can be used to generate an intricate structure:

Imagine, for instance, a language with an alphabet that contains three characters: F, +, and −. To create a Koch curve, we establish the following *production rules:* successive generations are obtained by replacing each F with F+F−−F+F, and leaving unchanged each + and −. Thus, starting with F, the first three generations develop as follows:

Generation 1:   F
Generation 2:   F+F−−F+F
Generation 3:   F+F−−F+F+F+F−−F+F−−F+F−−F+F+F+F−−F+F

It is quite clear that a complicated expression can be achieved from a simple one by applying and reapplying the production rules that define the grammar.

To produce an image, each element in the string can be taken as an instruction for a plotter. For example, F instructs the plotter to move forward a fixed distance while drawing a line; + instructs the plotter to turn to the left by 60 degrees; and − instructs the plotter to turn to the right by 60 degrees. After many generations, the resulting string, when plotted, will produce the snowflake pattern.

Grammars have been developed that instruct the computer how to form complex structures such as trees. Individual elements represent branch length, branch angle, and number of leaves. Starting with a branch of a certain length and inclination, with a given amount of foliage, the grammar determines what will happen next. For instance, if a branch is short, low-angled, and relatively leafless, the grammar might dictate in the next iteration that it be lengthened, raised to a higher pitch, and filled in with leaves. Carefully selected production rules and a range of different initial conditions can automatically create endless variations of the same tree. Each version will be unique, but they will all share identical principles of growth.

PHYSICAL MODELING

To simulate nonbiological phenomena in nature, computer scientists have put physical laws into their simulated worlds by incorporating the fundamental laws of Newtonian physics into their modeling procedures. Remember that particle systems do not necessarily need to obey physical laws. For example, in the simulation of the waterfall, the particles are created with a certain trajectory and lifespan that only simulates an aspect of the underlying dynamics. In the case of *physical modeling,* on the other hand, the computer is used to simulate the genuine laws of physics.

COMPUTER-GENERATED WILDFLOWERS These figures demonstrate computer simulation, through grammar-based modeling, of the growth of a single plant (*Lychnis coronaria*) and its profusion in a field. The top illustration shows aerial and side views of an individual plant at twelve stages of growth. The bottom image is a grammar-based simulation of the growth and development of red, white, and blue varieties of the same plant that have, initially, been randomly distributed. After seeding, the individual plants compete for space, leading to the separation of surviving, mature plants. The lower figure thus demonstrates how the simulation has modeled emergent properties of plant populations, such as the competition for scarce resources. Grammar-based modeling techniques are useful for characterizing the interaction of highly parallel systems and are thus well suited to modeling biological growth and development.

Consider, for example, the problem of modeling a toy jack as it bounces down a flight of stairs. Imitating the jack's fall might be possible simply by moving it through successive frames of a conventional animation, where each frame represents a moment in time. Of course, the animator might have difficulty making the jack bounce naturally. The sequence of frames would likely require many adjustments before the motion had a realistic appearance.

The process of generating a sequence of frames depicting this motion can be entirely automated, however, by mathematically describing the

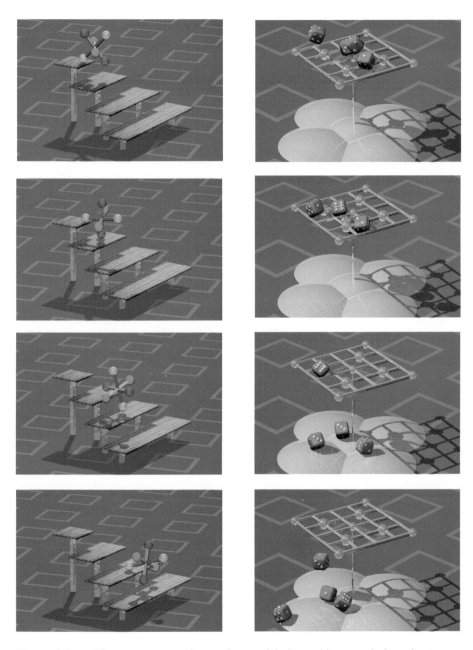

NEWTON'S LAWS The computer can be used to model physical laws, including classical mechanics, as shown here. The dice and the jack are obeying Newton's laws of motion as they tumble in these two computer-generated series by David Baraff of Pixar Animation Studios.

physical interaction of the jack and the stairs. To do this, variables such as mass and moments of inertia, familiar from elementary mechanics, are used to describe the jack. Given a description of the position and momentum of the jack for a given point in time, the computer can determine the position and momentum at successive moments using Newton's laws, as the jack bounces from step to step. These positions can be rendered as a sequence of frames that will play as an animation.

Computer simulation drives home the fact that Newton's laws are active everywhere and must be accounted for when we model even mundane phenomena. For example, the concept of a catenary needs to be understood before the drape of cloth can be modeled. A catenary is a seemingly simple curve of a suspended cable at equilibrium between the force of gravity and the tension holding the cable to its suspension points. Cloth can be modeled, at least approximately, as a mesh of catenaries, and mathematics can be used to describe their interaction. Each crossing of threads creates a kind of suspension point.

But to represent the drape of cloth accurately, modelers need to do more than calculate catenaries. Relying on the catenary alone implies that there is no rigidity to the threads between suspension points. In the real world, threads are not infinitely flexible. Burlap and denim, for example, are more rigid than silk and nylon. Cloth modeled using catenaries alone often appears too silky, and it is difficult to model more rigid textiles.

Physically based modeling gives us a sense of the complicated ways in which physical forces are operating all around us. It is difficult to simulate accurately all of these forces, but fortunately we have an able apprentice in the computer.

A Visual Experiment Some of the most commonplace phenomena of everyday life present formidable modeling challenges. This image depicts the character from the Academy Award–winning animation *Geri's Game* by Pixar Animation Studios. One of the most impressive technical achievements of this film is the natural way in which the old man's suit behaves as he moves. The suit is modeled as a surface with a variety of qualities, including stiffness, shininess, and seam placement. The computer scientists and artists that collaborated on this film adjusted these parameters with the objective of producing natural-looking movement in the rendered sequence. This cycle of adjusting parameters and viewing the resulting images is a kind of visual experiment, where the appearance of the clothing determines the best model.

PROCEDURAL SHADING

The efficiencies achieved with procedural methods can also be applied to the problem of simulating light in the computer. In all of the descriptions of rendering in Chapter 3, "Artificial Perspective," the geometry of the scene, however intricate, was fixed first, and only then was the computer used to simulate light. The illumination models described in Chapter 3 are parametric models—systems of equations with various parameters such as surface ambient reflectance, diffuse reflectance, and specular reflectance, and the spectral power distribution of the illumination. Scattered light is calculated by evaluating the equations.

In the case of *procedural shading,* the computer generates values for surface reflectance, illumination, and their interaction by following certain repetitive procedures at the time an object is rendered. Imagine, for example, modeling a block of wood or a vase carved from marble. The surface reflectance could be modeled one pixel at a time with an artist determining the appearance of the marble or by applying a two-dimensional texture map taken from a photograph. A problem arises, however, because the

COMBINING PROCEDURES Biomechanics, physically based modeling, and behavioral modeling are here combined to simulate the activity of fish in this frame from an animation. Biomechanics model the musculature and the body movement of the fish. To simulate swimming, the physical interaction of fins and water is modeled. Behavioral modeling is used to simulate the interaction of the fish with food, neighbors, and predators. By employing a variety of procedural graphics techniques, the computer has created a compelling imitation of an intricate, undersea world.

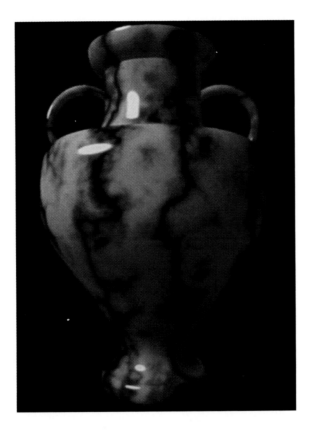

CLASSIC VASE Procedural shading has been used to determine the surface reflectance for each point in the three-dimensional volume from which this vase has been sculpted. In this landmark 1985 image by Ken Perlin of New York University, the computer follows a procedure to produce a marbling pattern that runs through the solid. If someone were to break off a piece of this model, the three-dimensionality of the pattern would be proven by the exposed cross section. Variations of this classic technique for producing random patterns are now prevalent in visual computing.

surfaces of the object should reveal a cross section of a three-dimensional pattern within the wood or marble. If we were to texture-map the grain of wood onto a rectangular block, it would give a false appearance of wrapping paper rather than planes cut through a three-dimensional pattern. Similarly, the interesting appearance of a marble vase derives, in part, from the way the surface exposes three-dimensional patterns in the marble.

To model the wood block or marble vase, we are left with the problem of finding the data to fill the three-dimensional texture. One might imagine slicing a real block of wood or marble into thin planes, each of which could then be digitally photographed. To determine the color of a surface point during rendering, the computer could then look up the value in a database of the digital photographs. This measured data, however, would only provide one particular example of wood or marble. It would be as if all objects were carved from the same block.

Alternatively, an endless variety of three-dimensional patterns can be generated procedurally. To create marble, for instance, the computer

HOW TO CREATE AN ANIMATED STAMPEDE Procedural methods are essential in the film and video industry because they free creative artists from the requirement that all objects be modeled realistically. Animators can use these techniques to produce stylized visual effects, whether it is the bounce in the step of an animated character or the long, mysterious shadows of a forest at dusk. Procedural methods have been one of the principal means by which computer graphics has lost its hard, crystalline appearance and has expressed a warmer, organic quality.

The wildebeest stampede in Disney's *The Lion King* is a compelling example of the use of procedural graphics in animation. The sequence probably would not have been undertaken in this form without procedural methods because it would have been too difficult to draw by hand. Traditionally, backgrounds are drawn with pen and ink and then colored. Moving elements or characters are drawn on plastic sheets, known as cels, which are superimposed over the background and photographed frame by frame to make an animated sequence.

Procedural methods have been developed for automating this painstaking process. Animating the herd of wildebeests required specifying both the position and behavior of each animal. The animators used a particle system to simulate the dynamics of the herd. The computer ensured that animals would not collide with or pass through one another and that the herd would follow a leader. The individual wildebeests were modeled in three dimensions, and they were also instructed to run and jump in three dimensions.

For many years, animators from the Walt Disney Studios have employed a characteristic shading style, one that audiences enjoy and associate with Disney productions. To create a final, computer-generated sequence that would match the rest of *The Lion King*, procedural shading techniques that imitate Disney's classic hand-animation style were developed for the three-dimensional wildebeest models.

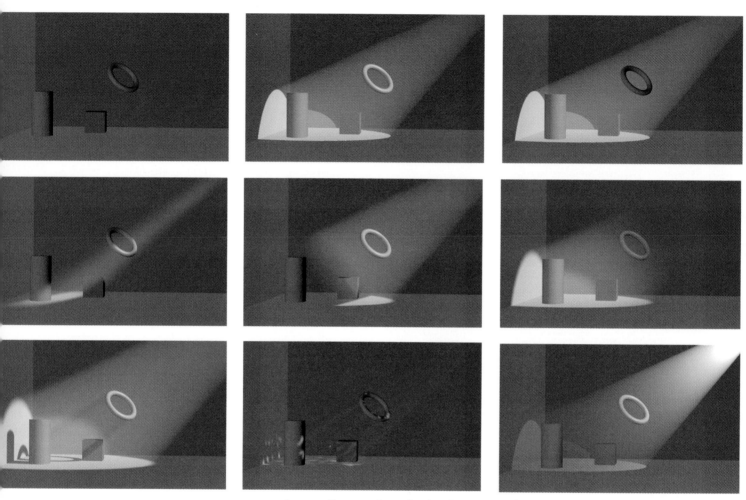

LIGHTING CONTROLS Procedural techniques are the ultimate tools for creating lighting effects. This series of images demonstrates how a procedural light source model can control the shape, falloff, spread, and texture of lights as well as the placement of shadows and other illumination qualities. *Left to right, top to bottom:* 1. Fill light only. 2. Spotlight added. 3. Spotlight does not illuminate torus. 4. Spotlight is elliptical. 5. Spotlight cuts off midway. 6. Spotlight starts midway. 7. Torus and cylinder cast shadow but cube does not. 8. Spotlight projects through texture. 9. Spotlight intensity attenuates with distance. All of these lighting effects could be generated manually, but the procedural technique gives a high degree of control to the computer graphics artist.

starts with a slowly varying random black-and-white pattern in three dimensions. It then successively adds other random patterns that vary more rapidly than the one that preceded it. After several iterations, a cloud-like, three-dimensional texture is generated that is reminiscent of the iterative patterns created with fractals. The result at every point is passed through a lookup table to convert this intermediate result to a color. Different lookup tables give different colors and widths of the marble veins, and different random patterns that are summed together produce different vein locations and shapes.

A three-dimensional wood pattern can also be computed procedurally. The computer can, for instance, mimic the distribution of rings in a tree by creating light and dark circular bands with random widths. The computer can perturb the bands from perfect circles, and it can make the radii of the rings a function of the distance along the axis of the tree, simulating how a tree may taper with height.

To eliminate unnecessary computation, calculating an entire volume of data to render the block of wood or marble vase is not actually necessary. Only the values of the texture at each point on the surfaces need be determined because no other parts of the volumes are visible. Rather than indexing a three-dimensional texture to find the color of the surface, the computer uses the procedure to compute the color of the surfaces from the location of the surface points in three dimensions. This is an advantage of procedural shading. It automates the generation of shading data while minimizing the amount of data that is required. Only the appearances of the visible surfaces need to be determined.

Procedural shading applies to all aspects of light in the computer, not simply the colors of surfaces. A surface can be given an embossed appearance, for instance, by procedurally perturbing its orientation at every point. The perturbations may be determined by the computer with a procedure or derived from a texture map, known as a *bump map,* for how it simulates bumpy surfaces.

Likewise, the angular distribution and falloff of a light source can be computed procedurally. To imitate the patterns of light reaching the floor of a forest, for example, sunlight may be attenuated by a procedure that, it is hoped, imitates the shadows created by the canopy of leaves. Similar strategies can be used to attenuate light to imitate fog, mist, or smoke.

One of the most significant advancements in computer graphics has been the development of special *shading languages* used to describe these kinds of lighting and shading procedures. Without these languages, the use of computer graphics for motion picture special effects would be severely restricted. Without shading languages, it would be impractical to create and render compelling computer-generated sequences, let alone entire computer-generated feature films. Shading languages have made it possible to simulate patchy fog, rain-slicked roads, scaly reptiles, herds of cartoon animals racing across plains, to say nothing of the seamless integration of computer-generated and live-action imagery. Shading languages represent functions and operations that can be combined in endless permutations to produce an ever-expanding repertoire of visual effects. As more and more procedures are developed, artists will have limitless ways in which to use these languages, not only to imitate reality, but also to expand our visual experience.

SIMULATION AND VISUAL COMPUTING

Procedural modeling borrows much from physics, biology, and other sciences. In visual computing, as we simulate, for instance, a toy bouncing down a flight of stairs or the drape of a cloth, we are visualizing the laws of physics. If rigidity is added to the model of the catenary, a very different-looking sort of cloth is modeled than one that is assumed to behave as a perfect catenary. Computer-generated plants have yet to be mistaken by a botanist for real plants, but they increasingly embody principles of growth and differentiation and are therefore worthy of the botanist's interest.

Visual computing affords computer scientists an opportunity to examine the assumptions of physical models visually. In the dialogue between model building and seeing, computer scientists have the chance to refine scientific models so that they reflect more of the complexity and richness of the natural world.

The creation-like narrative of the history of visual computing is not simply a chronology of better-and-better-looking images. The pursuit of naturalism sometimes requires understanding more than appearances. Renaissance painters, wishing to depict the human form, found it necessary to dissect the human body to understand the underlying anatomy. In piercing the flesh, they blurred the distinction between art and science.

Something akin to this is happening in visual computing on a rather grand scale. In the quest for realism, computer scientists have had to study nature in all of its intricacy. The tools have been developed to model growth, differentiation, behavior, energy flow, and physical dynamics—indeed to model almost any natural phenomenon. Visual computing in this sense has moved beyond image making. As we will see in Chapter 6, "Beyond Appearances," the line between visual computing and computer simulation is beginning to blur.

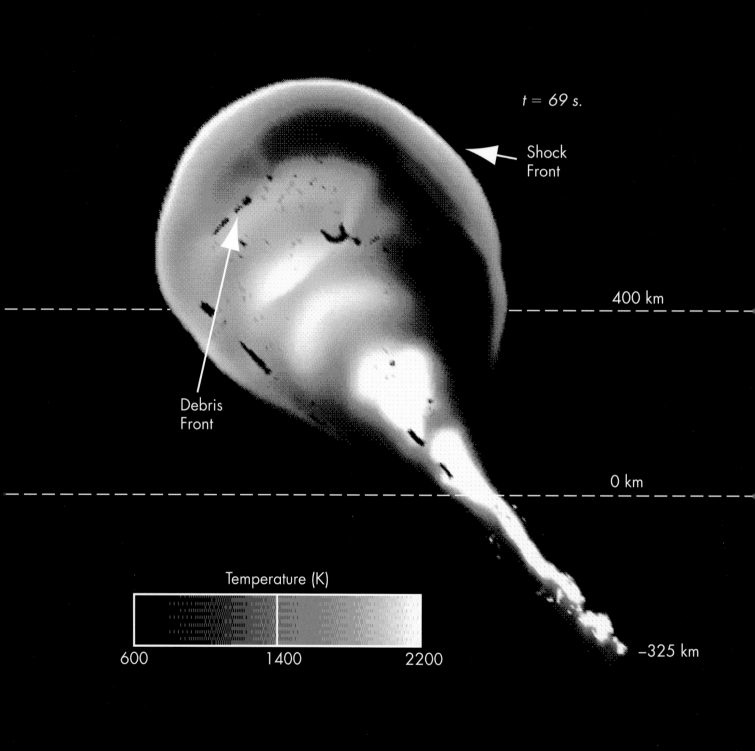

$t = 69\ s.$

Shock
Front

400 km

Debris
Front

0 km

Temperature (K)

600   1400   2200

−325 km

Beyond Appearances
6

The psychical entities which seem to serve as elements in thought are [not words and language but] certain signs and more or less clear images which can be "voluntarily" reproduced and combined. This combinatory play seems to be the essential feature in productive thought—before there is any connection with logical construction in words or other kinds of signs which can be communicated to others. The above mentioned elements are, in my case, of visual and some of muscular type. Conventional words or other signs have to be sought for laboriously only in a secondary stage, when the mentioned associative play is sufficiently established and can be reproduced at will.

—*Albert Einstein*

PERCEIVING COMPUTATION This visualization of a fireball resulting from the collision of the comet Shoemaker-Levy 9 with Jupiter was rendered from data from a supercomputer simulation. The lower altitude indicated by a dotted line (0 kilometers) is Jupiter's cloud cover, and the upper dotted line indicates the altitude (400 kilometers) at which the fireball would be visible from Earth. Visualization is an essential tool for interpreting large volumes of data produced by computer simulations. A common feature of visualizations from many scientific, engineering, medical, and design disciplines is the manner in which imagery engages perceptual processes to form a close coupling between the human thinker and the prodigious computational power of machines.

It is a testament to the intimate connection between vision and thought that subtle visual observations can have profound scientific implications. Thus an electron can be inferred from the thin vapor trail of a cloud chamber, and the wave nature of light can be deduced from the minute bands produced by light passing through adjacent pinholes. Similarly, an unexpected shadow on a photographic plate led Roentgen to the discovery of X-rays.

In this same spirit, in 1993 in the Arizona desert, three astronomers, Eugene and Carolyn Shoemaker and David Levy, detected a comet in a few grains of silver. As is usual for comet watchers, the astronomers photographed the sky nightly searching for anomalies, the appearance of a small spot that, moving from night to night, would become apparent in the superimposition of photographs. The comet they discovered that night, later named Shoemaker-Levy 9, was of titanic size and devastating energy. Luckily, Shoemaker-Levy 9 was headed not for Earth, but for Jupiter.

The final year of life of Shoemaker-Levy 9 created an unprecedented opportunity for the emerging field of scientific visualization. In earlier chapters, we have seen how the computer can be used to model the interaction of light and surface and how the drive for realism led to modeling the dynamics of nature. *Scientific visualization* takes this an important step further, joining the modeling power of computers with image synthesis so that physical processes can be analyzed visually.

Scientific visualization came to maturity in the years before the appearance of Shoemaker-Levy 9, driven by the promise of a whole new way of doing scientific experimentation using a computer. Computer graphics is used to make imagery representing a simulation so that scientists can visually interact with their models. Among the phenomena that scientists using visualization have explored are thunderstorms, the evolution of galaxies, and the circulation of blood. The benefit of scientific visualization is greater than simply saving the time and trouble of real-world experiments. Indeed, visualization is a way of advancing sophisticated mathematical models at warp speed.

Like any new field, however, visualization has its skeptics. Some scientists argue that simulating physical phenomena in the computer will not yield results that stand up in the real world. As Shoemaker-Levy 9 hurtled toward Jupiter, scientists seized the chance to test the validity of visualization. The comet's collision with the mighty cloud-covered planet was a unique occasion to check a computer simulation against empirical data. Observations made with Earth-based and space-based telescopes could be used to check the accuracy of the computer models.

Shoemaker-Levy 9 broke into several masses as it encountered Jupiter's gravity. There were many important questions: How deep would the fragments of Shoemaker-Levy 9 penetrate? What kinds of shock waves would be produced by the impact? Would it be feasible to model a comet without exact information regarding its composition?

Astrophysicists at many institutions around the world were eager to simulate the collision, to take on the challenge of foreseeing this truly cosmic event. Some predicted shock waves with a force of millions of megatons and 1,000-mile-high fireballs. Others expected the impacts to amount to nothing more than a large meteor shower that would disintegrate as it descended into the Jovian atmosphere.

SIMULATING A COMET IMPACT

A team of impact scientists at Sandia National Laboratories—David Crawford, Mark Boslough, Timothy Trucano, and Allen Robinson— developed some of the most detailed simulations of comet Shoemaker-Levy 9. When reduced to its fundamentals, however, their mathematical model was based on the simple idea that the dynamics of the collision would be similar to that of a pebble dropped into a still pond.

The stillness of a pond indicates that an equilibrium has been established between gravity and molecular interactions. When the water is still, the system is at its lowest possible energy state. The impact of the pebble forces apart the loose bonds among the molecules. Momentarily, the equilibrium is disrupted, and the water is placed into a higher-energy state as it absorbs the energy of the pebble. As the system returns to the lower-energy state of equilibrium, it typically throws off a droplet of water.

By analogy, the Sandia team expected the collisions to result in the ejection of massive fireballs from the Jovian atmosphere. The term *fireball* is meant loosely, because the hot gas is not really on fire but does carry a large amount of heat and mechanical energy. The computer model was used to predict the size, location, and shape of the fireballs, questions that taxed the limits of their supercomputer.

As the actual mass of the comet was unknown, the research team ran simulations of the fireballs using a variety of sizes and densities. The scientists used *computational fluid dynamics,* a family of mathematical techniques that model the physics of fluids. The density, temperature, velocity, and pressure of the Jovian atmosphere were calculated as a function of time and as a function of the velocity and size of comet fragments. To make the model as accurate as possible, even the chemical reactions that would be triggered in such high-energy conditions were simulated.

The magnitude of the problem precluded simulating the entire collision of each fragment with Jupiter in three dimensions. In computational modeling, such as that done in fluid dynamics, the term *resolution* refers to the fineness of a computational grid, a set of points mapped onto the system for which the computer will calculate the physical quantities. The initial penetration of the fragments into the atmosphere needed to be modeled at very high resolution because the fragments were expected to break into small pieces. Because the required resolution of the model was very fine in this case, it was inconceivable that even the world's fastest supercomputer could be used to calculate all points in three dimensions in any practical amount of time. Fortunately, it could be safely assumed that the dynamics of the comet's penetration would be radially symmetric and, therefore, a two-dimensional model would suffice.

The fireballs, on the other hand, were expected to be asymmetric because of the oblique trajectories of the comet fragments, relative to Jupiter's gravitational pull and atmospheric pressure. This asymmetry required that the generation and ejection of the fireballs be modeled in three dimensions. Fortunately, it was also reasonable to reduce the resolution of the model for the fireballs, to use a lower-resolution computational grid, because fine structure would not be needed.

NUMBERS AS IMAGES

The sheer volume of data produced by such simulations creates a profound problem of interpretation. If the numerical output were in the form of stacks of paper filling a warehouse, the data from this simulation would be indecipherable and the model would be useless. However complex the underlying computations, the Jupiter simulation, nonetheless, represents the movement of matter and energy in three spatial dimensions. Therefore, a movie can be made to represent the dynamics of this system. To convert numbers into images, the Sandia researchers applied the tools of computer graphics described in the earlier chapters.

The Sandia team was not able to predict accurately what would happen at the time of impact because the density and precise composition of the comet were unknown. Their approach to this problem was to play

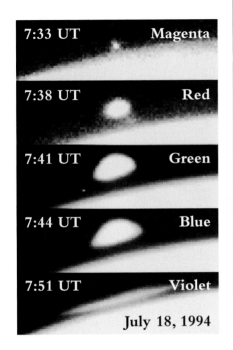

7:33 UT	Magenta
7:38 UT	Red
7:41 UT	Green
7:44 UT	Blue
7:51 UT	Violet

July 18, 1994

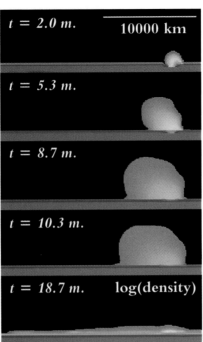

$t = 2.0\ m.$ 10000 km

$t = 5.3\ m.$

$t = 8.7\ m.$

$t = 10.3\ m.$

$t = 18.7\ m.$ log(density)

SIMULATION AND OBSERVATION Images of one Shoemaker-Levy 9 fireball from the Hubble Space Telescope (left column) are compared with images from a computer simulation (right column). A number of differences between telescope and simulation images complicates their direct visual comparison. The Hubble photographed the comet impact through a series of filters, as indicated. In the computer simulation color represents the log density of the gas, whereas the Hubble is measuring light emanating from and reflected by the fireball. Nonetheless, comparison of the columns indicates that the evolution of the simulation roughly matches the actual fireball.

out a range of densities and to produce a range of possible collision scenarios. This, it should be said, was not the same as "betting on all the horses" because telescopic observations would provide insight into whether any of the simulations, at least qualitatively, matched the observed fireball ejection.

The Sandia team used a variety of visual computing algorithms to depict the fireball. *Volume rendering,* for example, was used to generate the image that opens this chapter. Volume rendering simulates the passage of light through a semitransparent medium. In this case, the opacity of the volume data is a function of pressure, and color encodes temperature. As can be seen, the shock wave is limited to a narrow region at the periphery of the fireball, with a relatively high temperature. Trailing the shock front is a debris front, containing material from the fireball and the Jovian atmosphere ejected by the impact.

The size of many of the actual fireballs, their asymmetric shape, their evolution over time, and the amount of ejecta they propelled into the sunlight appearing over the Jovian horizon proved to be quite consistent with the Sandia simulations. In the figure on this page, for example,

PERCEPTUAL DIMENSIONS This series of images, from a simulation of the collision of two neutron stars by David Bock at the National Center for Supercomputing Applications, demonstrates the way in which perceptual dimensions can be related to the dimensions of a scientific data set. The top image is a volume rendering of the entire data set, where color indicates neutron density with blue representing the lowest and yellow the highest density. The surfaces depicted in the middle image represent boundaries between high and low densities of neutrons. The cylindrical arms are an example of the way in which the visual system extracts shape from shading, a form of depth perception. The bottom image, a slice through the data, uses color to denote the highest densities (pink and red) within the same volume.

Color is a perceptual dimension with a high degree of independence of shape from shading so that sharp boundaries and high densities can be simultaneously depicted in the same image with minimal conflict between perceptual dimensions. Thus, the figure on the opposite page, which combines all three images, depicts the interior densities of this neutron star collision with significant boundaries and surrounding low-density matter. This volume visualization was created using procedural lighting and shading as described in the previous chapter. Visualization requires an understanding of the different properties of the submodalities of visual perception to represent data effectively.

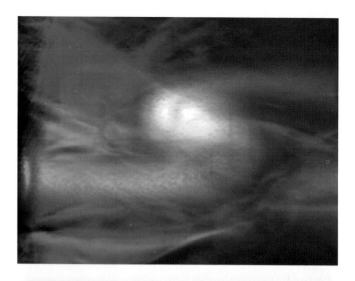

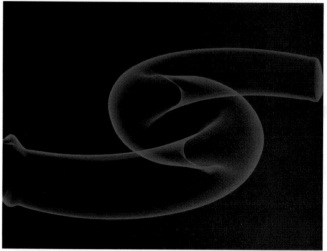

observations made by the Hubble Space Telescope of the impact of one fragment are compared to simulation images. Color in the visualization is used to represent the density of material. As can be seen, there are both similarities and differences between the computed and observed data.

Making images from numbers is rarely an automatic process. If the data is complicated, if it depicts the interaction of several variables, thoughtful consideration must be given to the best representational strategy. The challenge is to optimize the match between data dimensions and the imperfectly independent dimensions of human vision. While human vision includes the three dimensions of space and the dimension of time, which are independent, there are also additional perceptual dimensions that can be utilized. For example, color, brightness, and shape can be used to convey information even though they are not completely independent of one another. It is a great challenge to represent simulations so that they can be readily understood, an issue addressed in the next chapter, and it often requires collaborations between artists and scientists.

As a test of computer modeling, the Shoemaker-Levy 9 simulations are quite instructive. It is clear from the whole effort to model the comet that computer simulation has a dialectical relationship with traditional, empirical science. Visualization has not turned out, in most instances, to divorce theory from measurement. The Sandia researchers had to run many simulations because they had only rough information about the mass and size of the comet fragments. They were able to fine-tune the theory from which their computer models are derived by comparing this range of simulations with the empirical observations. The comet simulations suggest that the computer is not so much a replacement for the laboratory as a medium to investigate the implications of mathematical models.

STEERING COMPUTATION

In modeling the impact of Shoemaker-Levy 9, there was little need to interact with the computer simulation as it unfolded. Although the Sandia group wanted to test a range of values for the comet's density in order to consider a range of conceivable scenarios for the impact, the output computation could be produced automatically once the input parameters had been specified. The path from initial to final conditions, even if quadrillions of computations were required, was predetermined.

But it is not always the case that the purpose of a simulation is to determine in an automatic way a set of output values. In many cases, the mathematical model is used to explore a dynamic relationship among interrelated variables, and all the tools of computer graphics can be used to help guide the process. This kind of *interactive* visualization necessitates both fast computation of the mathematical model and extremely rapid graphics. This practice of modifying the direction of a computer model as it is being calculated is sometimes referred to as *steering* a computation.

Computational steering is essential for simulating the dynamics of molecules. Chemists are interested in molecular geometry because it determines molecular function. Biochemists designing drugs are frequently trying to create molecules that bind to so-called active sites on target molecules. This process is often compared to that of a lock and key. A hormone, or other messenger molecule, binds to an active site, thereby triggering a biological process. The messenger molecule is the key that turns the active site lock, initiating a more extended biochemical event.

There are two basic strategies for modifying this lock-and-key phenomenon. One approach is to block the action of an endogenous molecule that binds to an active site and turns on biological processes that are pathogenic. This might be done by creating an analogue to the endogenous molecule that will bind to the active site but not, so to speak, "turn the key." A second approach is to imitate the action of a molecule that is underrepresented or nonexistent in the body. In this case the biochemist wishes to synthesize a molecule that will function as a key, binding to the active site of another molecule in a manner that will trigger a beneficial biological process.

In both cases, the biochemist is trying to get a good fit by relating the geometry of the proposed molecule to the geometry of the active site on the target molecule. Biological molecules generally are composed of one or more strings of amino acids, and it is the sequence of amino acids that determines its structure. It is difficult, however, to predict the stable configurations, the *conformations,* that will form for complex molecules. The atomic forces between the amino acid groups in a molecule generally will cause the molecule to fold in upon itself in order to reach a more stable conformation with a lower potential energy.

INTERACTIVE GRAPHICS To steer a computation visually the computer must be able to render images very quickly. In template forcing, for example, the computer must generate images as quickly as the scientist can conceptualize. To achieve this kind of real-time interaction, computer scientists have developed specialized computer architectures and algorithms that accelerate computer graphic rendering.

One of the most widely used methods for accelerating graphics is called polygon rendering. As noted in Chapter 3, "Artificial Perspective," objects with flat surfaces can be modeled with polygons while curved surfaces can be approximated with polygonal meshes. Polygons are well-suited for accelerated systems because they can be projected from the scene directly onto the image plane with perspective geometry. This kind of projection, reminiscent of Alhazen and Alberti, is equivalent to tracing a line from each vertex to the viewpoint to determine where it intersects the image plane.

A simple way of making an image is to connect the projected vertices with lines, a so-called wireframe representation. The righthand portion of the figure below is a wireframe representation of a model of the Roman Colosseum. If a design is quite simple, a wireframe may be a fully sufficient representation. To engage additional perceptual competencies, however, the model should have shading and surface texture. Specialized computer architectures have been developed that rapidly fill in pixels within the projected image polygons with these image qualities. Pixel brightnesses within the polygons in the middle of the figure are computed with a local illumination model that calculates ambient, diffuse, and specular reflection from simulated light sources. On the left side of the figure, the computer additionally associates the model polygon with a piece of texture in a two-dimensional texture map and applies that texture onto the image polygon.

Although polygon rendering uses local illumination models and, therefore, does not faithfully model the full environment of light, it is advantageous because images can be calculated so quickly. For example, we can fly over this model of the Colosseum in real time. The aerial view shown on the opposite page depicts the building as originally constructed.

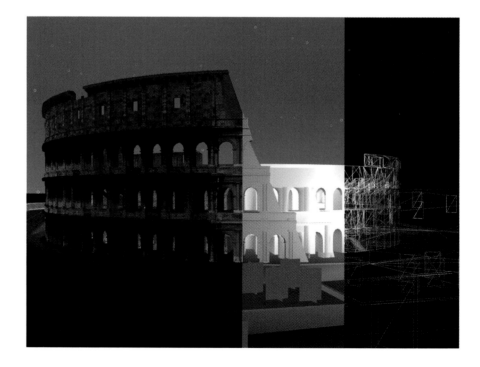

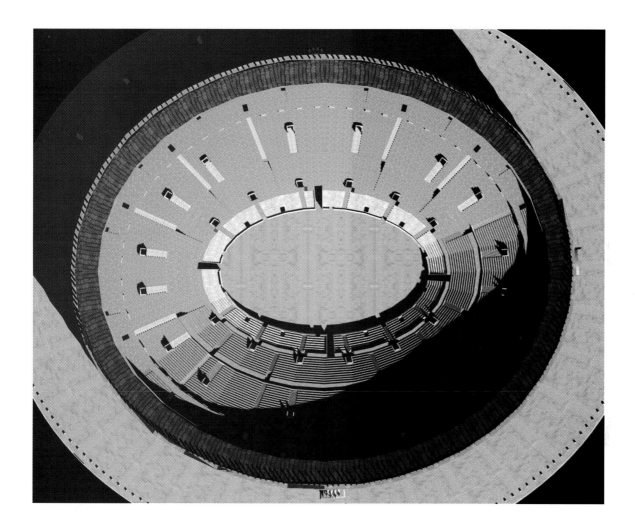

A tremendous amount of computation is required to determine likely stable conformations. A relatively modest biomolecule can have tens of thousands of atoms all interacting with several interatomic forces. Without the computer, a biochemist would be forced to predict the conformation of a molecule by working with a physical model such as those made from balls and sticks. The biochemist would try to calculate the potential energy of various conformations in an effort to understand the likely folding among the various amino acid chains. Even with the aid of a fast calculator, however, the ball-and-stick method can be impractical, particularly for large molecules.

Template Forcing

The visual computer has revolutionized molecular modeling. One technique called *template forcing* enables the biochemist to interact visually with molecular geometries to determine the most stable conformations. A molecule is manipulated through a visual interaction while the value for its potential energy is simultaneously calculated in an accompanying window. As the molecule is forced into different configurations, billions or trillions of arithmetic calculations are executed in real time. Template forcing is powerful because it allows a chemist to observe molecular behavior step by step. In order for two molecules to bond, they need to reconfigure their geometries, a process that cannot go forward if it requires too much energy. Through the interaction with the computer, the biochemist can explore various scenarios by which the molecule might reconform to bond with an active site.

Pharmaceutical researchers Charles Bugg, William Carson, and John Montgomery used template forcing to develop an inhibitor for the enzyme purine nucleoside phosphorylase, or PNP, as shown in the illustration. PNP suppresses excessive T-cell activity associated with diseases such as multiple sclerosis, diabetes, and rheumatoid arthritis. A number of PNP inhibitors have been developed, but most have proven to be more effective in the laboratory than in the human body. The most potent compounds are too large to pass through cell membranes, while small molecules have, for unknown reasons, lacked efficacy.

The biochemists focused on filling three distinct regions within the PNP active site. The problem was not simple because many molecules have the requisite gross geometry. The computer enabled the scientists, however, to explore in detail the molecular bonds that would be formed for a large number of candidates. It is an iterative process by which the chemists quickly identified the key molecular components that were required for an ideal inhibitor.

Visual computing greatly accelerates the speed at which drugs can be proposed and evaluated. Research that took ten or fifteen years in the past can sometimes be completed in only a few years with these techniques. Furthermore, the laboratory simulated in the computer, with the aid of scientific visualization, can produce better final products because the chemical bonds that form between the drug molecules and the active sites are much better understood.

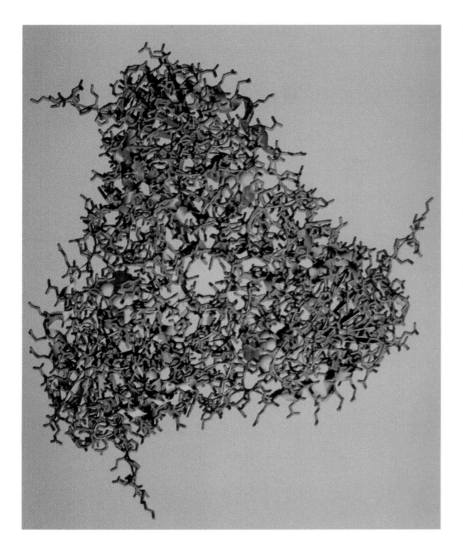

DESIGNING DRUGS The full structure of the molecule purine nucleoside phosphorylase (PNP) is shown in this computer model with constituent atoms denoted by color. There are three identical lobes organized around a central axis. An active site in each of the lobes is filled with the normal substances that PNP acts upon, a purine nucleoside and a phosphate ion shown as large spheres. PNP, however, is also known to act upon some drugs intended for the treatment of disease. Researchers, therefore, are using computer simulation to search for a drug that inhibits the activity of PNP.

MOLECULAR STRUCTURE AND FUNCTION The figure on the following page shows a close-up of a computer model of PNP and a putative inhibitor. The PNP is represented by blue spheres while the inhibitor is represented by multicolored spheres. The computer permits the biochemist to interactively test compounds for their geometrical fit with the active site of an enzyme. New molecules can be created and tested in the computer quickly so that the biochemist has the experience of "steering" towards an optimum fit between inhibitor and active site. This inhibitor of PNP is targeted for the treatment of arthritis.

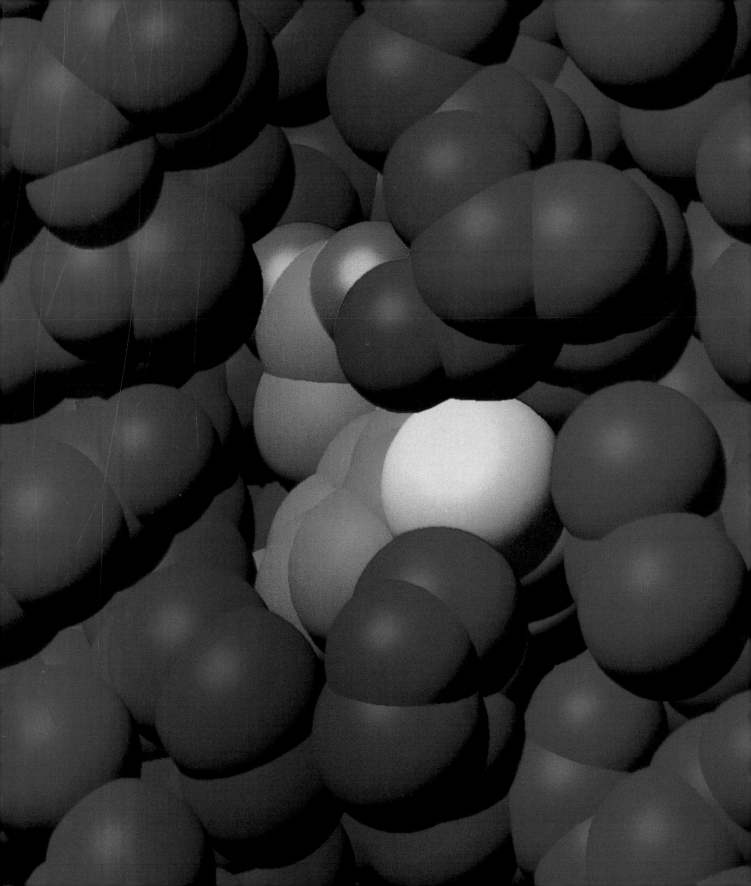

It is instructive to consider how visual computing with template forcing has restructured the problem of molecular design. Without the computer, molecular conformations must be envisioned in the mind of the scientist, perhaps with the aid of physical models. The scientist's activity, therefore, is divided between constructing three-dimensional mental models, each with its particular potential energy, and evaluating the way in which the resulting conformations will fit the active site. With visualization, on the other hand, the task of relating potential energy to conformation is shifted to the computer. Conformation geometry is rendered with computer graphics and interpreted by the scientist visually. Conscious thought can then be focused on making judgments regarding the match between lock and key.

Computational steering is not only used in biochemistry. For example, an aeronautical engineer might interactively modify an airplane wing while simulated smoke trails show the resulting changes in aerodynamics. Likewise, automobile manufacturers can test where the greatest strains will occur in a crash and how a car will crumple. Indeed, the major manufacturers of automobiles have been among the most active proponents of visual computing. In automotive modeling, engineers evaluating the safety of a

ENGAGING VISUAL COMPETENCIES In molecular modeling, computer-generated images are based on modeling interatomic forces, while in flight, simulation images are rendered from models of aircraft dynamics and terrain. Although these are very different kinds of simulations, both represent an intimate fusion between human thinking and the vast computational power of the computer that is mediated through visual imagery. In both cases, in order to create the closest coupling of thinking and computation, images are computed with color, lighting, perspective, motion, and texture cues that are intended to engage the full range of visual competencies. The challenge of flight simulation is to create this high level of realism in real time. This image, from an interactive simulation, shows a Stealth fighter flying over an airfield toward the ocean. The terrain is a texture map derived from a high-resolution photograph.

Here the Stealth fighter is flying over the ocean with three other aircraft. The ocean includes representations of waves and other details generated with texture-mapping techniques.

car use the database created by the design engineers. The safety and design engineers use visual computing to analyze the same data to solve different problems, contributing an extraordinary gain in efficiency to the whole process of producing a high-quality finished automobile.

Computational steering allows a much freer exploration of the relationship between form and function. Just as with chemical modeling, the computer makes it possible to investigate a wider range of options, a process that is mediated by all of the previously discussed techniques of modeling and shading. The use of visual computing employs the human visual system for tasks that would otherwise require conscious mediation. This shift enables the designer to move among alternative scenarios with great ease and, thus, is powerful support for the creative process. This is undoubtedly why visual computing has found its way into almost every area of design.

A VIRTUAL SOLUTION SET

In computational steering, the computer, coupled with the human visual system, makes it possible to explore a much larger part of the problem

The Stealth now approaches an airfield at night, rendered as it would appear through infrared-sensitive night vision goggles. Modeling infrared light is different than modeling a sunlit scene. With infrared modeling, the source of the light is principally the objects themselves. For a high level of realism, the computer model also accounts for the nonlinear properties of the night vision system. Flight simulation is a particularly demanding environment requiring rapid generation of realistic images, but the same techniques are increasingly used in other disciplines to support a close coupling of computing and human thinking.

space than would otherwise be possible. All possible solutions to a problem can be thought of as points located in N-space where N is the number of variables. If N-space is too large to compute, the computer is used to create a *virtual solution set*. A virtual solution set is achieved when the computer can calculate alternative solutions extremely quickly, and the graphical interface is used to locate specific regions of interest in N-space. If the interface is truly interactive, the user has the experience of every possible solution to the problem coexisting simultaneously.

No matter what is being designed—a new automobile or a new drug molecule—the number of alternative possibilities can be extremely large and, in fact, incomputable. Without the computer, the designer can spend a lot of time heading in directions that may not be workable. The automotive designer may design a fender styling that is not structurally sound or that is too heavy. The molecular designer may find that a conformation forms an unanticipated bond with a nonactive site. In short, without the computer the exploration of the solution set is inefficient. The computer accelerates the speed at which alternatives can be explored and can quickly help eliminate excursions toward inadequate solutions.

SIMULATING A ZEBRA ROOM Automotive manufacturers traditionally have relied upon "zebra rooms" to judge surface fairness, the degree to which an automobile surface conforms to design specifications. In a zebra room, a full-scale physical model is illuminated by an array of parallel light tubes so that a design engineer can study the reflected pattern. The contours of the stripes indicate surface curvature, and imperfections are often evident in disruptions of the pattern.

The zebra room technique relies upon human visual sensitivity to linearity and motion. This zebra room is computer simulated and is an example of using the computer to create images that can be easily interpreted by engineers familiar with traditional techniques. The three-dimensional model of the automobile is rendered with environment mapping, where the environment map is a pattern much like the illumination in a real zebra room. (Three-dimensional model courtesy of Milai Corporation, Japan.)

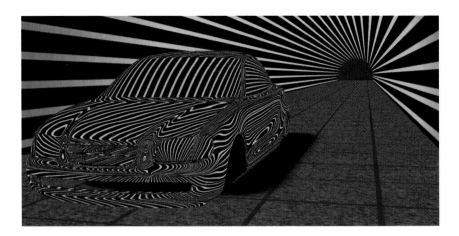

MIND AND COMPUTER

One cannot go very far in the field of scientific visualization without wondering about the union between mind and computer formed by computer graphics. There was a time, when the field was young, when it was tempting to think that visualization was effective simply because of the obvious power of human vision.

Vision is, after all, the sense that most directly connects us with the external world. It is vision which, through high-powered telescopes, connects us with the most distant reaches of the universe. Vision, through medical instruments and microscopes, forms our understanding of the workings of the body and the cell. We build visual models of atoms and molecules and even of light itself using the analogy of waves and particles.

In the early years of visual computing, the nature of our relationship with the computer was hardly understood. It was often said that the "enormous bandwidth" of the human visual system was sufficient justification for computer visualization. Computer simulations were said to produce fire-hose sprays of data that could not be apprehended without exploiting this tremendously wide channel. But if vision is a channel, where does the enormous amount of information go?

The proliferation of visualization into so many fields requires a fresh look at this new kind of interaction between humans and machines. On the computer side of the interface, high-speed processors can perform trillions of calculations per second. Human beings cannot, however, process the output of such computations directly. The computations must be first converted, with a massive amount of additional computation, into a form that can be understood by a human perceiver.

More and more scientists are finding that the best way to do this is to convert data into shapes, colors, and textures, which are rich stimuli for a visual system adapted, as it happens, to an entirely different problem. The product of the computation must be translated into the language of a visual system that creates our visual world from patterns of light. Shading algorithms are used to tangle up nonexistent computer-generated object surfaces with nonexistent computer-generated light so that the confounded message can be presented to a visual system that inherently requires such confounded messages. The whole spectacle becomes surreal when the simulation has no actual visual dimension, as in the case of a black hole or a magnetic bottle. How extraordinary to transmit the computer simulation of these nonvisual phenomena to human consciousness through vision!

The closed loop of visualization raises one of the most intriguing questions in science. For all of our keen interest in vision and the great research effort that has been made, we still really do not know how the retinal patterns become the conscious experience of seeing. We know from physiological and psychophysical studies that the visual system is constituted of a great army of parallel analyzers that each attack different bits of the scene. These processes are said to be *preconscious* because they occur quite separately from *conscious* thinking, indeed in entirely different regions of the brain and even in the retina itself.

We do not know, however, how those millions of separate acts achieve unity in a single, visual world. We only know that our conscious experience of sight depends upon the computational achievement of this other, quite massive, part of the human brain.

With all of this going on, the processing of great armies of neurons, the seamless union between thinking and computation achieved with visualization is a pleasure to contemplate. Machine computation is converted, at great expense, to imagery that is projected to the retinas. The imagery is then deconstructed by a massive parallel processor in the human brain so that it can be understood by consciousness, which in turn influences the machine computation again.

In this context, it will not do to explain this process away with talk of the bandwidth of the human visual system. Of course vision is powerful, but what is happening to the information the visual system is processing? As we shall see in the next chapter, it is the dialogue between two very different human competencies, thinking and seeing, and between two distinctly different regions of the human brain, that is relevant and that has relentlessly driven the invention of ever-more-powerful visual computers.

Conscious and Preconscious
7

VISUAL UNDERSTANDING Images, whether computer generated or not, can reallocate information processing needed to solve a problem from conscious intellection to preconscious visual processes. This geological survey of Southern England by William Smith (1769–1839) depicts geological strata with different colors so that they can be instantly understood without much conscious analysis. The map, which did much to stimulate interest in the geological sciences in the early nineteenth century, summarizes a large quantity of data collected by Smith over a long career walking throughout England. His data would be difficult to understand if presented in a less visual form, for example, as notations in notebooks. The visual computer can employ many additional visual modalities and can directly translate complex empirical data or simulations into imagery, but the shift from conscious to preconscious is much the same.

The psychic activities that lead us to infer that there in front of us at a certain place is a certain object of a certain character, are generally not conscious activities, but unconscious ones. In their result they are equivalent to a *conclusion*. . . . But what seems to differentiate them from a conclusion . . . is that a conclusion is an act of conscious thought. An astronomer, for example, comes to real conclusions of this sort, when he computes the positions of the stars in space, their distances, etc., from the perspective images he has had of them at various times and as they are seen from different parts of the orbit of the earth. His conclusions are based on conscious knowledge of the laws of optics. In the ordinary acts of vision this knowledge of optics is lacking. [P]sychic acts of ordinary perception [may be thought of] as *unconscious conclusions,* thereby making a distinction of some sort between them and the so-called conscious conclusions.
— *Hermann Helmholtz*

In vision science one does not always need a sophisticated instrument to perform experiments with great scientific and philosophical implications. An ingenious stimulus, perhaps just a printed pattern, can provide the enjoyable experience of seeing one's own visual system in action. The right kind of image can be every bit as powerful as the scalpel or electrodes of the physiologist in revealing the workings of the machinery that converts ephemeral patterns of light into a visual world.

THE RANDOM DOT STEREOGRAM

The random dot stereogram is one of these delightful and illuminating probes, and it is used here to help explain something important about visual computing. With the random dot stereogram, we can perform an armchair experiment that demonstrates how visual computing changes the way we solve problems. To participate in our experiment, try comparing the left and right patterns in the figure on the facing page to see if you can determine how they differ. You may not have the patience to compare the left and right patterns in every detail, and it is not necessary to do so to appreciate the significance of this experiment. Rest assured, however, that there are differences, and it is worth a few moments of your time to try to discover them.

Many people, when asked to do a comparison, move up and down the columns, checking each square against its correspondent in the other image. Most people find this process quite tedious.

There is another way to solve this problem, one that is much more rapid and enjoyable, but you will have to use an entirely different part of your brain. If the two images are fused stereoscopically, a central T-shaped area will appear above the page. The T shape floats above the background because of differences between the left and right patterns—differences you attempted to discover by inspection.

The random dot stereogram was developed by Bela Julesz at Bell Laboratories to study binocular depth perception. It is easy to make a random dot stereogram. In this example, two copies of a random pattern have been generated, one for the right eye and one for the left eye. The patterns are identical except for a small T-shaped area in the middle. In the left image, this central area is shifted to the right, and in the right image, the same area is shifted to the left.

TWO WAYS TO SOLVE A PROBLEM The difference between the left and right patterns above can be detected either with conscious thinking or with preconscious visual processes that operate without conscious awareness. As an exercise, it is well worth trying to detect the difference between the left and right patterns by comparing corresponding squares. It quickly becomes apparent that the serial method of looking back and forth between the left and right patterns, square by square, is fatiguing and time-consuming.

Alternatively, the two images can be viewed stereoscopically so that the left image is projected to the left eye and the right image is projected to the right eye. With stereoscopic viewing, a central "T" shape, more than half the height of the whole image area, will float above the background. The floating region is the perceptual product of a visual subsense responsible for binocular depth perception called stereopis which builds a depth world based on the disparity between the left and right retinal patterns. The floating T is an area within the otherwise identical patterns that has been shifted, relative to the background, left in the right image and right in the left image. This horizontal shifting simulates a property of our visual world wherein, from the perspective of our left and right eyes, closer objects are shifted right and left, respectively, relative to the background.

When the two patterns are stereoscopically fused, the task of comparing them is moved from conscious inspection to this preconscious visual subsense. The serial operation of comparing the two patterns square for square using conscious thinking has been exchanged for a preconscious operation that is based on highly parallel processors that mediate the earliest stages of visual perception. Accompanying this shift is a big gain in efficiency. Designers of scientific visualizations and of graphical interfaces succeed when they are able to exchange conscious, serial processing for preconscious, parallel processing in this manner.

To fuse the stereo pair, it is necessary to view the left image with the left eye and the right image with the right eye. This takes some practice to do without a stereoscopic viewer, but the effort is worthwhile. It helps to hold a piece of cardboard vertically between the two images so that each eye is presented with only one image. By relaxing your eyes, the two views can be made to merge in the center.

The T shape appears to float above the background when the patterns are fused stereoscopically because we have visual machinery specifically designed to detect differences between left-eye and right-eye images. Our binocular perception of depth is a consequence of *stereopsis* (Greek, meaning *solid sight*), a depth perception subsense that detects this kind of textural disparity. If the left-eye image of a natural scene were compared to the right-eye image of the same scene, it would be observed that objects are horizontally displaced to the left in the right image and to the right in the left image relative to their common background. The nearer the objects, the greater the horizontal disparity. Stereopsis correlates the left-eye and right-eye images based purely on their textural properties; it does not depend on the recognition of objects. Indeed, the random dot stereogram is just a random pattern. There are no objects in the scene, only disparity between the two patterns. We do not need to activate the machinery of stereopsis consciously. Ever the loyal adjutant, this process starts looking for correlations between the retinal patterns without our conscious awareness, contributing an important component to our visual experience.

The random dot stereogram has been an important stimulus for understanding stereopsis, but that is not its relevance here. In participating in this informal experiment, you have had the opportunity to experience two very different modes of problem solving, one utilizing conscious processes and the other using preconscious processes. The first attempt to detect the differences between the left and right patterns by inspection was dependent on conscious thinking. The second attempt using stereopsis moved this information processing task to the preconscious processes of the visual system.

This shift from conscious to preconscious helps to explain why computing is becoming ever more visual. Generally speaking, visual computing transfers information-processing challenges from conscious to preconscious processes. It should be noted, however, that by *pre*conscious we do not mean *un*conscious, the psychoanalytical concepts that describe repressed wishes and hidden motives in human thinking. Preconscious visual mechanisms are the genetically determined and developmentally fixed processes of the visual system. Scientists are often in a position that is analogous, whether they realize it or not, to a process of moving back and forth between the left and right members of the random dot stereogram. They may be flipping pages of numerical output to analyze a computer simulation or recalculating potential-energy values for a molecule. When scientists are engaged in such repetitive serial tasks, those calculations can often be moved to preconscious processing and executed in parallel with the help of a visual computer.

Let's look more closely at the nature of the shift from conscious to preconscious processing. When you tried to consciously determine the disparities between the left and right patterns of the random dot stereogram you, as it were, improvised a serial algorithm. You no doubt

MAPPING DATA TO PERCEPTUAL DIMENSIONS Psychophysical and physiological studies have indicated that separate analytic pathways of the visual system contribute different components to our visual experience. Visual subsenses responsible for recognizing objects through form and color, for example, are different than those responsible for analyzing motion and stereoscopic depth. In visual computing, therefore, it is imperative that the different competencies of visual perception be understood and respected.

Margaret Livingstone of the Harvard University Medical School has suggested that a poorly chosen color scheme in a visualization can produce conflicting messages among the visual pathways. This can be demonstrated by making a shaded image *equiluminant.* In a shaded image,

form is perceived from changes in luminance. To make an image equiluminant, colors are used that have equal brightnesses. We still see color in the image, but the visual analysis of form based on shading is confounded. For example, if we make one of Leonardo's drapery studies (see Chapter 2) equiluminant, the depth in the image disappears, and we are left with a flat pattern of colors.

The psychophysically differentiable subsenses of vision have varying degrees of independence from one another. For example, humans can perceive three spatial dimensions monocularly, and they are highly independent. On the other hand, stereoscopic depth perception interacts with monocular depth perception and, so, cannot be considered a fourth, fully independent dimension. Similarly, color is largely independent of depth perception, but brightness perception and color influence each other.

Computer scientists are gradually developing strategies by which multivariate data can be mapped to perceptual dimensions. Since perceptual dimensions are not entirely independent, this task can be challenging. Generally speaking, it is advisable to use color to represent data that fall into discreet categories, so-called nominal data. Quantitative dimensions are usually best mapped to the three spatial dimensions. One way of representing ordinal data, data that represent an ordered list, is with brightness. We can distinguish ordinal differences in brightness, but it is difficult to distinguish quantitative differences. As useful as these guidelines are, the translation of multivariate data into images that can be fully understood preconsciously remains as much an art as a science.

looked back and forth between the left and right images to determine if a particular location was the same in both images and repeated this process over and over again in serial fashion. Preconscious visual processes, by contrast, are massively parallel. When you viewed the random dot stereogram stereoscopically, a large number of parallel visual processors worked on the problem simultaneously.

There are some interesting distinctions to be made between conscious-serial and preconscious-parallel processing. The serial method is much slower than the parallel method, and is much more tiring. The serial method requires improvising a procedure by which the left and right members of the pair are compared: it requires an *ad-hoc* algorithm of one kind or another. The parallel method, on the other hand, is automatic, all but indefatigable, and mediated by analytical systems that are hard-wired or, at least, organized early in visual development.

Given the great power of these preconscious processors, one might wonder why humans need lumbering, improvised, and easily fatigued conscious processes at all. The subject of consciousness has been investigated since the beginning of philosophy, and this question is obviously difficult to answer. Certainly, one virtue of conscious processes is that they are flexible. While parallel processors are fast, they are fixed in their functioning. Conscious processes can be modified continuously and can perform much more sophisticated analyses than preconscious ones.

VISUAL EXPERIMENTS

The shift from conscious to preconscious processes is quite evident in scientific visualization. The purpose of scientific visualization, indeed of all forms of scientific experimentation, is to explore the interplay between independent and dependent variables. Independent variables are controlled by the experimenter while dependent variables are observed. A successful experiment reveals the relationship between the two.

In the Shoemaker-Levy 9 comet impact simulation developed at Sandia Laboratories, for example (see Chapter 6), the independent variables were the size and density of incoming comet fragments. These variables were independent because the actual sizes of the fragments were unknown. In successive simulations, the scientists could vary these independent variables and observe their effects on the dependent variables, for example the fireball behavior, fragment penetration depth, shock-wave temperature, and shock-wave speed.

Computer graphics enabled the comet impact researchers to depict the dependent variables in a manner that could be easily interpreted preconsciously. A simulation was translated into an animated sequence that depicted the impact of the comet. Imagine trying to determine the relationship between the independent and the dependent variables without a computer. Conscious thinking would be required to translate the output numbers, in some manner, into a "mental image." Analyzing the tremendous quantity of numerical output for meaningful patterns would require so much effort that it would be difficult, if not impossible, to address the main question of interest: the effect of the independent upon the dependent variables. With visualization, conscious thinking is, instead, devoted to the task of analyzing the relationship between the independent and dependent variables.

Here, just as with our random dot stereogram experiment, serial conscious processes give way to parallel preconscious processes when visualization transfers the burden of information processing from the conscious to the preconscious domain. Without the computer, conscious thinking would have to be devoted to many repetitive computations, and the task of relating the independent variables to dependent variables would have to be improvised as a series of steps in thought. With visualization, the computations are handled by the computer, and the dependent variables are *instantly* perceived.

Much the same can be said about template forcing, the visualization technique in biochemistry also described in the previous chapter. Without visualization, conscious thinking is required to relate an independent variable, molecular conformation, to a dependent variable, potential energy. With visualization, the molecule can be conformed at will while potential energy is displayed visually. Once again, there is a replacement of a conscious mental process, some sort of *ad-hoc* serial algorithm, with fast, tireless preconscious processes.

Visualization restructures a problem by substituting preconscious visual competencies and machine computation for conscious thinking. Visualization is, therefore, useful whenever the impact of an independent variable on a dependent variable can be perceived preconsciously. In a successful visualization, conscious thinking can be directed at probing the relationship between the independent and dependent variables without distraction.

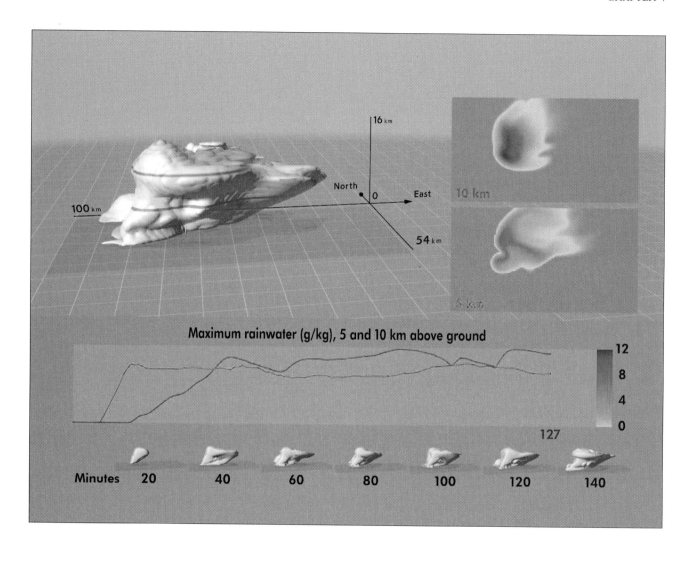

Maximum rainwater (g/kg), 5 and 10 km above ground

In many other nonscientific fields where visual computing is used, there is a similar shift of information processing from conscious to preconscious. We may not think of an automotive engineer's or an architect's design work as an experiment in the normal scientific sense, but if the work is performed on a visual computer, the benefits can be much the same as in visualization. Instead of building prototypes, the automotive engineer uses a computer because the design can be modified much more easily. If the engineer varies the shape of the body, the computer can automatically calculate and represent aerodynamics, weight, and cost as well

VISUALIZATION OF A THUNDERSTORM The visualization of the relationship between a large number of variables requires a careful mapping to perceptual dimensions to shift as much information processing as possible from conscious to preconscious. This visualization of the formation and evolution of a thunderstorm represents the data from a supercomputer simulation from the National Center for Supercomputing Applications. The visualization was done by Colleen Bushell, Matthew Arrott, and Michael McNeill of NCSA and Edward Tufte of Yale University. There are five variables represented in the visualization. The four independent variables are time and the three dimensions of space, and the dependent variable is the density of rainwater.

The upper-left-hand figure is a volume visualization in which a critical transitional value in density is represented as a three-dimensional shaded surface. The shading enables the perceiver instantly to understand an aspect of the density preconsciously. The right-hand pair of figures are horizontal cross sections through the volume at 5-kilometer (purple) and 10-kilometer (green) altitudes. In the cross sections, density is represented by a brightness scale from white to dark blue-green, a scale that minimizes perceptual artifacts because the chosen colors form a smooth continuum of brightnesses as shown in the scale on the bottom right. The volume visualization is a single frame from an animation, which shows the evolution of density with the passage of time. Density versus time is represented in the bottom of the figure in two different ways. The graph represents the maximum rainwater density at altitudes of 5 and 10 kilometers, again represented by purple and green, respectively. The seven small volume visualizations give a general sense of the changing spatial distribution of density over the same time period.

This visualization efficiently maps information to perceptual dimensions. In the volume visualization, quantitative distribution of density takes advantage of our ability to judge the three dimensions of space quantitatively. The two-dimensional cross sections rely upon brightness judgments and are best considered an ordinal representation because our ability to judge brightness is not truly quantitative. Purple and green colors are used deftly as nominal categories. Density, as it changes with time, is also mapped to a spatial dimension, a horizontal axis in the graph, and the series of volume visualizations.

Understanding the numerical output from this simulation would be very difficult, if not impossible, without its being represented as imagery. Therefore, the visualization represents a massive shift of the information processing required to understand the simulation from conscious to preconscious processes. Additionally, the sophistication of the mapping to perceptual dimensions avoids many perceptual artifacts that would require conscious thinking to correct.

as component manufacturability. Similarly, an architect can add a story to a building and instantly know the impact on the building schedule, the usable space, the energy requirements, and the cost of construction. In both cases, conscious thinking can be directed to the relationship of an independent and a dependent variable in an undistracted manner.

THE COMPUTER SCIENTIST AND THE PSYCHOPHYSICIST

The examples of visualization above, as well as the experiment with the random dot stereogram, illustrate the idea that there is a dichotomy between processes that are consciously directed and processes that are in some sense preconscious. We have approached this distinction in

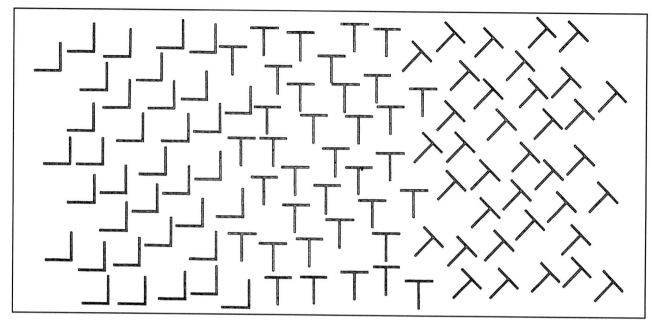

PREATTENTIVE PROCESSES This illustration suggests a difference between preattentive and higher-level visual processes. A border is immediately evident between the vertical T's in the center area and the tilted T's populating the right third of the figure. A closer look reveals another border between the left-most third of the figure and the center area. The right-hand border "pops out," because low-level analyzers that operate in parallel across the entire scene can detect the differences between the middle and right thirds of the figure. These low-level processors apparently cannot detect the difference between the middle and left portions of the figure. The ability to see the left-hand transition requires serial comparison of individual elements by a higher process. Visual psychophysicists have used stimuli of this kind to test the properties of low-level, presumably parallel analyzers. In this case, the analyzers are assumed to be particularly sensitive to line orientation.

qualitative terms. Conscious thinking, the stream of thought, is a familiar subjective phenomenon, and preconscious processing has been loosely defined as something that does not interrupt this experience. The question arises: Can we define preconscious processing more precisely?

Vision scientists tend to use the term *preattentive*, rather than *preconscious*, to characterize low-level visual processing. The term *preconscious* is better suited for visualization because it focuses on the distinction between conscious processing and processes that are not mediated consciously such as (but not limited to) preattentive processes as they are defined by visual psychophysicists presently.

The figure above by Jacob Beck of Boston University helps to clarify the distinction between preconscious and preattentive. It contains both a boundary that is visible and one that is not immediately apparent. The boundary that is immediately visible is formed by the border between the vertical and tilted T's scattered across, respectively, the middle and right thirds of the figure. Closer inspection, however, reveals another border separating the left-most third of the figure—an area constituted of right angles. The question asked by the visual psychophysicist is why perception of one of the borders requires serial inspection, comparing elements on both sides of the border, while the other simply pops out. What does Beck's figure tell us about preattentive visual competencies?

Vision scientists tend to think of the earliest stages of vision as mediated by a sea of individual analyzers, operating in parallel, each concerned with a tiny portion of the scene. These analyzers are thought to operate autonomously and can signal the presence of a specific feature. Presumably, the tilted T's trigger a different response by these early analyzers than the vertical T's, while the right angles and vertical T's trigger identical responses. The result is that we see, without conscious effort or serial inspection, a conspicuous border between the tilted and vertical T's, but we see no discontinuity between the right angles and the vertical T's until we inspect the scene more closely.

From Beck's figure, we cannot be sure what the critical difference is between the tilted and vertical T's but it seems relevant that the right angles and vertical T's are both constituted of similarly oriented elements. It would appear that line orientation might be a critical feature for these low-level preattentive analyzers.

Starting with just this simple figure and the idea of a array of parallel analyzers, we have the makings of a model of the first stages of vision. The model, which is undoubtedly an oversimplification, includes low-level processors and a higher level of analysis, sometimes called a *spotlight* of attention, that detects features that do not trigger the lower level analyzers. There seem to be two processes, a *preattentive* process, which would appear to be sensitive to limited kinds of textural features, and an *attentive* process, which can perform more complicated analyses but, perhaps, in a more serial fashion.

In the 1980s, Anne Treisman, a psychophysicist at the University of California at Berkeley, used this distinction between features that are undetectable to low-level vision and those that pop out to develop a methodology to assess the specific competencies of preattentive vision. Her reasoning was that if a target can be distinguished from other elements, distractors, by these parallel analyzers, the search time required to find it should not be influenced significantly by the quantity of distractors.

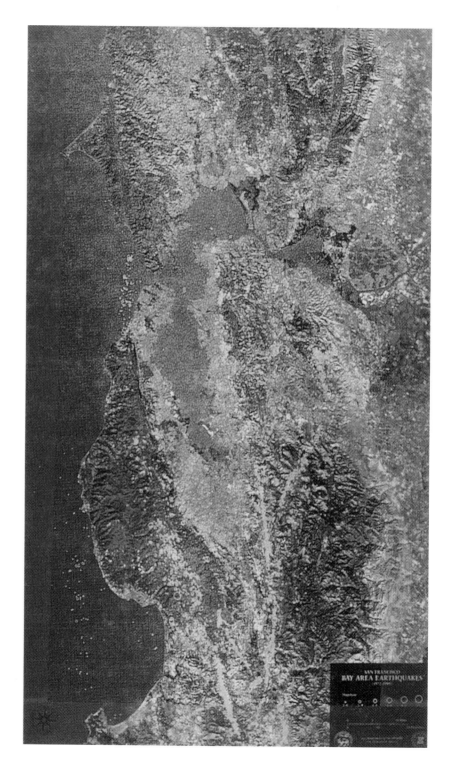

VISUALIZING EMPIRICAL DATA Not all computer visualization is based on three-dimensional simulations. This infrared satellite image from the U.S. Geological Survey depicts San Francisco Bay Area earthquakes from 1972 to 1989. Earthquake epicenters are represented by yellow circles, where radius represents the magnitude of the quake (see legend). The size scale used for the circles has been adjusted so that dense areas blend together and depict yellow fault lines. The fault lines perceived in this image could also be identified by sifting through numeric data, although it would be a challenging task. The image shifts this burden to preconscious processes, so the information is instantly understandable. The quality of a visualization can be judged by whether values of the dependent variable, in this case the magnitude of earthquakes, can be understood without distracting serial, conscious analysis.

Since the analyzers are thought to be working in parallel, the target, the element that triggers a preattentive response, should trigger a response instantly, even if it is hidden among a large number of distractor elements. If the target requires attentive processing, however, the kind of processing that presumably creates the border between the T's and right angles in Beck's figure, the search time required to find the target should increase with each added distractor because many elements need to be inspected.

When the target differs from the distractors in orientation, curvature, or color, the target stimulus is detected in the same amount of time whether there are just a few distractors or dozens. The target simply pops out because it triggers low-level feature detectors. If the target is defined by a conjunction of these properties, however, the search time will lengthen with the addition of each distractor. The time required to identify a red O target hidden among red N with green O distractors will depend on the number of distractors, presumably because the target is defined by a conjunction of two elementary properties—in this case, curvature and color—both present in the distractors.

Search time is undoubtedly a powerful tool for investigating features that trigger the earliest stages of visual processing. Color, size, contrast, tilt, curvature, line ends, three-dimensionality, the direction of lighting, movement, and stereoscopic depth are all properties of targets that will pop out. Targets that combine these attributes increase search time and therefore are thought to require a different kind of visual analysis. Since Treisman's earliest experiments, the distinction between strictly parallel and strictly serial processes has begun to blur, and visual psychophysicists are developing more sophisticated models of preattentive vision. Nonetheless, Treisman's method has done much to illuminate the workings of early vision and is the groundwork for more comprehensive models.

PRECONSCIOUS VERSUS PREATTENTIVE

Unlike psychophysicists, computer scientists have the luxury of being able to utilize visual competencies without the need to understand precisely how they work. Computer scientists are thinking more and more of visualization, and all visual interaction with the computer, as an opportunity to exchange conscious thought for information processing that occurs in the preconscious domain.

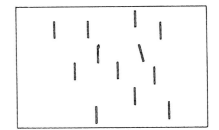

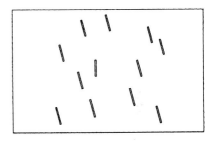

POPPING OUT Anne Treisman has developed a methodology for investigating the features available to hypothesized, parallel preattentive analyzers. Her test is based on the idea that features that can be distinguished preattentively do not require serial visual searching. In the top figure, the tilted target "pops out" from a field of vertical distractors. This popping out occurs even if the number of distractors is increased substantially, suggesting that the analysis that distinguishes the target occurs in parallel across the entire scene. In the bottom figure, the target and distractors are reversed, and the single vertical element does not pop out from a field of tilted distractors. Presumably, preattentive parallel processors involved in early visual analysis are particularly sensitive to changes from the vertical. Although early visual search processes may not be exclusively parallel or serial, these experiments do hint at the features used by the earliest, predominantly parallel stages of vision.

Vision is, after all, a system of interacting subsenses that are dependent on the same external receptor, the retina, but which have very different capacities and make different contributions to our visual world. The subsense responsible for color processes information differently than stereopsis, which processes depth information from textural comparisons of left-eye and right-eye images. Stereopsis, in turn, extracts different features from the retinal patterns than subsenses responsible for *monocular* depth, which may utilize shadows, occlusion, perspective, and other features of the scene. The texture and motion of our visual world is dependent upon still other subsenses.

The computer scientist views vision from the top down, starting with high-level intellectual processes used for solving abstract problems. The vision scientist, on the other hand, concerned with preattentive vision,

LIGHT AND EARLY VISION One might assume that preattentive visual search is based only on elementary two-dimensional features. This figure by James Enns and Ronald Rensink of the University of British Columbia suggests, however, that parallel searching can also utilize information about the three-dimensional geometry of elements as well as the direction of lighting. As noted earlier, our interpretation of three-dimensional geometry appears to be closely coupled with illumination judgments. In the top figure, an anomalous target stands out from a field of distractors that collectively support a top-down illuminant. The distractor appears either as a black-topped box also illuminated from above or a side-illuminated element. Either way, the visual processes that distinguish the target from distractors appear to be preattentive. In the bottom figure, the target and distractors have been exchanged. In this case, the target does not pop out, presumably because the field of distractors does not support a top-down illumination model as effectively. Experiments such as these suggest that the separation of light and surface must begin in the earliest preattentive stages of visual analysis and affirm the importance of using carefully nuanced shading and illumination cues to optimize the shift from conscious to preconscious in visualization.

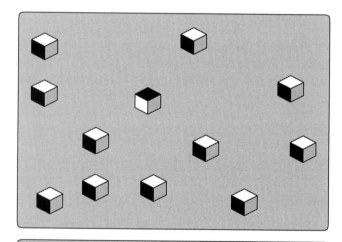

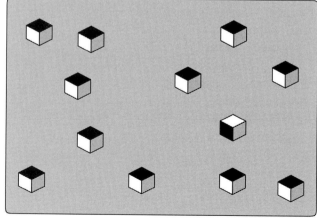

approaches vision from the bottom up. Preconscious processes, therefore, can be seen as a superset of preattentive processes. Indeed, there are preconscious competencies that seem quite far afield from the Treisman-type preattentive feature detectors. The interpretation of symbols, for example, is not hard-wired. We learn to recognize stop signs, maps, or even letters on a printed page. As you read these lines, the pattern is translated without your conscious awareness into meanings through an elaborate interpretive process that you learned in school. The process that translates the pattern on this page into words lies outside your train of thought and, so, would qualify as preconscious but it is quite unlike the preattentive processes described by Treisman. The term *preconscious,* therefore, is meant to encompass all visual processes that do not seem to be manifestly consciously mediated.

Even the most familiar interactions with the computer are made more efficient and more enjoyable if they are handled preconsciously. A graphical interface is superior to an alphanumeric interface because the graphical interface does not interrupt your train of thought. In the old days of computing, much of the user's conscious attention was devoted to typing and executing arcane commands. Now, most of the administrative tasks associated with computing are done preconsciously, by pointing and clicking symbols. Indeed, the great explosion in the use of the Internet occurred only after an interface was developed that made it possible to access its basic functions with preconscious competencies. Connecting computers was not enough to create a revolution in communication. The revolution only occurred after a computer interface was invented that took into account, in a certain sense, the architecture of the human mind. The basic functionality of the Internet existed from its earliest days but would not become commonly used until it could be mediated preconsciously.

The more that is known about the different subsenses of visual perception, and the manner in which they interact to produce our visual world, the more effectively computer scientists can use all the tools of graphical computing to facilitate a true union between thinking and computing. As the field of visual computing moves forward, practitioners should be mindful of the great differences between thinking and seeing. To achieve a fusion between machine computation and thinking, visual computing scientists must be clever about making full use of vision, of these extraordinary preconscious processes. Indeed, we might be guided by a simple motto: Never use conscious processes to perceive!

Epilogue

I can see more and more clearly that I will have to work very hard to render what I am looking for: the instantaneous impression, particularly the envelope of things, the same all-pervading light.
— *Claude Monet*

To the completely detached observer, there is irony in the idea of adapting powerful computers to simulate the interaction of light and surfaces so that the two can be properly confounded in an image. The proverbial "visitors from another planet," perhaps with a more direct perception of objects than ours, might find it odd to see some of our most advanced technology adapted to such a seemingly negative purpose. To understand visual computing, they would first need familiarity with the nature of human vision. They would need to know that, in our everyday world, we continuously reckon with a barrage of intensities that strike our retinas, that this entangled message is, improbably, factored into our own synthesized world of surfaces and something else, an immaterial quantity enveloping surfaces, that we call light. The aliens would be keen to discover that this light of human perception has a distant and difficult-to-define connection with electromagnetic energies of a certain range of wavelengths, a form of energy with which they would surely be familiar.

HAYSTACKS, END OF SUMMER (1891) Claude Monet.

It has taken some time to reach the view that this enveloping quantity is a sublime gift, a part of ourselves, rather than an impersonal feature of the physical world. Undoubtedly, the first inklings about the nature of light belonged to the earliest artists interested in imitating with pigments what they saw. By necessity, they would have discovered that lifelike pictures could not be satisfactorily rendered from pigments taken directly from the depicted objects and that more faithful pictures required a palette of colors unlike the literal colors of their subjects. In these informal experiments, light and subject began to separate, and light itself was something to paint.

Such was the collision of natural philosophy and art in the fifteenth century, with such a premium placed on mirroring reality, that it was inevitable that there would be an intense interest in light. The great geniuses of the Renaissance, including Michelangelo, Leonardo, Raphael, and Brunelleschi, worked to decipher the code, to understand the rules by which pigments could be used to represent light. At times, as in Raphael's paintings, the idea of using a material pigment in this way, of depicting with matter that which is manifestly immaterial, took on a spiritual aspect. The suggestion of light with pigment became a central imperative of the visual arts, a prime measure of the artist.

Given the worship of perspective and the realistic depiction of light in Western art after the Renaissance, it might not seem surprising that the invention of photography in the nineteenth century would shake things up. Photography in itself is something of a miracle, if you stop to think about it, and it must have unsettled artists to learn that the cherished ideals of painting could be achieved partly by an automatic, photochemical process. The threat, however, proved to be a spur. Photography has had manifold influences on painters, including an interest in perception. Impressionists realized that light is not out there in the world but is in the eye of the beholder. They took it upon themselves to study, not the physical world, but our perception of it. To their credit, impressionists enjoyed perception for its own sake. They savored a paradox others might find quite troubling, that we see only a world we create.

Such is the background that computer scientists faced in our own time as they made their first tentative steps toward using the computer, not simply to make images, but to imitate the interplay of light and surface. Many of the pioneers in these early efforts were aware of the difficulty of their undertaking from study of the masters. Looking back, it is interesting to see that dissatisfaction with the images computer scientists synthesized drove them to connect with the problems contemplated for so long by painters.

To the art historian or painter, the algorithms and procedures of computer scientists might seem soulless. Confronted with a history of art going back to cave dwellings, it is sometimes difficult to disagree. But something quite important is going on in visual computing. We are rediscovering visual reality from the ground up. The computer is being adapted to the singularly human way of thinking and perceiving. And while visual computing may take a long while to acquire a proper soul, as painting has, computer scientists are, algorithm by algorithm, opening a passage between thinking and computing that has unlimited possibilities.

ACKNOWLEDGMENTS

The ideas in this book were developed over several years of investigation and valuable interactions with researchers in the fields of visual computing, vision science, and art history. In this regard, we would especially like to thank Professor Pat Hanrahan of Stanford University for extensive conversations, insight, and inspiration. In addition, we would like to thank Margaret Livingstone, Torsten Wiesel, Jim Schirillo, Janis Mann, and Paolo Berdini. We would like to thank everyone listed in the image credits for graciously providing wonderful illustrations, including those who created images exclusively for this work: Chikai Ohazama and Matt Pharr.

We also would like to thank all the people at W. H. Freeman and Company who helped to bring this book into existence, including, but not limited to, Philip McCaffrey, Christopher Miragliotta, Vivien Weiss, Jennifer MacMillan, Hilary Hinzmann, Susan Moran, and Jonathan Cobb.

Finally, part of the formula for an enjoyable experience writing a book is to have warm and supportive relationships from one's friends, family, and colleagues. In this connection, Richard would like to express his appreciation to Mike Burns; Ray Dolby; Claudia Duarte; Phil and Jennifer DuBois; Teri Edelstein; Steve Forshay; Arnold and Frances Friedhoff; Lawrence, Beth, Emily, Jane, and Sarah Friedhoff; Carey Goldberg; June Goodfield; Bill Jasper; Alan and Cricket Jones; Nathaniel Kahn; Jay Scarpetti; Ed and Shiho Schummer; Giancarlo Poli; Nancy Walsh; Vivian Walworth; Joe White; and Karen Gilbert. Mark would like to thank: Paul and Catherine Peercy; Michael Peercy and Suzanne Kuo; the HFG; Brian Cabral; Peter Ostrin; David Blythe; Dan Baum; and Danny Loh.

Sources of Illustrations

Frontispiece *A Man Seated Reading at a Table in a Lofty Room* by Rembrandt (1606–1669)/The National Gallery, London

Facing page 1 *The Geographer* by Jan Vermeer van Delft (1632–1675)/Artothek, Peissenberg, Germany

Page 3 *Computerworld* (1967) Volume 1, No. 14. Courtesy of Robert A. Goldstein

Page 4 Edwin Catmull/Pixar Animation Studios

Page 5 top right, Pixar Animation Studios
bottom, Rendered using Lightscape © 1996 Umlaut (Paris, France)
top left, Based upon the rendering technology of Gary Demos, Frank Crow, and Jim Blinn. © 1978 Gary Demos and Information International

Page 7 Image from *Making Waves* (supplement to the video *Outside In* © 1994 The Geometry Center). Courtesy of A. K. Peters, Ltd.

Page 9 Mark Peercy/SGI. Volume data courtesy of Kenji Ono/Nissan Research Center, Japan

Page 10 *Sacral-Idyllic Landscape from Pompeii* (c. 62–79 C.E.)/Scala/Art Resource

Page 14 *Madonna and Child with Saints* by Andrea Mantegna (c. 1430/1–1506 C.E.) National Gallery, London

Page 15 *Seated Figure* by Leonardo da Vinci (1452–1519)/The Louvre. Scala/Art Resource

Page 18 Rowland Institute for Science. Courtesy of Julius J. Scarpetti

Page 23 Greg Ward Larson, LBNL. Original radiance map by Paul Debevec, UCB

Page 24 Mark Peercy/SGI

Page 27 *The Daughters of Edward Darley Boit* by John Singer Sargent (1856–1925). Gift of Mary Louisa Boit, Julia Overing Boit, Jane Hubbard Boit, and Florence D. Boit in memory of their father, Edward Darley Boit. Courtesy, Museum of Fine Arts, Boston

Pages 28–30 Mark Peercy/SGI

Page 32 *The School of Athens* by Raphael (1453–1520) Stanza della Segnatura, Vatican Palace, Vatican State. Scala/Art Resource

Page 35 Artist drawing a model in foreshortening through a frame using a grid system by Albrecht Dürer (1471–1528). Woodcut from *The Art of Measurement* (Nuremberg, 1527). (B. 149) Private Collection. Foto Marburg/Art Resource

Pages 37, 40–43, 45, 47–49, 51 Geometry, Mark Peercy/SGI and Matt Pharr/Stanford University. Rendered by Matt Pharr/Stanford University

Page 39 Corbis

Page 53 Chiostro by Joshua Rosen. Rendered with Lightscape 1996

Page 56 Courtesy of Doug Johnstone, University of Toronto and STScI

Page 59 Astrology Team, U.S. Geological Survey, Flagstaff, Arizona

Page 60 Paul Haeberli/SGI

Pages 62–63 Jet Propulsion Laboratory/NASA

Page 64 *A View of Delft, with a Musical Instrument Seller's Stall,* by Carel Fabritius (1622–1654)/The National Gallery, London

Page 65 Paul Debevec, University of California at Berkeley

Page 66 Chikai Ohazama and Mark Peercy/SGI. Geospecific data courtesy of Remote Sensing Laboratories, University of Zurich, and the Swiss Federal Office of Topography

Pages 68–69 Patrick Hanrahan and Marc Levoy, Stanford University

Page 70 Culver Pictures

Page 72 Barbara Meier, Walt Disney Feature Animation

Page 75 Duncan Brinsmead, Alias/Wavefront. Image created using Power Animator

Page 77 Craig W. Reynolds. http://www.red.com/cwr/boids.html

Page 78 Mark Peercy/SGI

Page 82 Przemyslaw Prusinkiewicz, University of Calgary

Page 83 Simulated and rendered at Cornell University, Program of Computer Graphics. Courtesy of David Baraff, Pixar Animation Studios

Page 85 Pixar Animation Studios

Page 86 Demetri Terzopoulos, University of Toronto

Page 87 Ken Perlin, New York University

Page 88 Image from *The Lion King* © Disney Enterprises, Inc.

Page 90 *Journal of Graphics Tools* 2(1): 1–20, 1997. Courtesy of Ronen Barzel

Pages 94 and 99 David A. Crawford, Sandia National Laboratory

Pages 100–101 Visualization by David Bock, NCSA Visualization Simulation by Doug Swesty, Alan Calder, and Ed Wang, NCSA and SUNY Stony Brook

Pages 104–105 Courtesy of Infobyte SpA-www.infobyte.it

Pages 107–108 C. Bugg et al., *Scientific American,* (1993) Vol. 269, No. 6, pages 92–98. Courtesy of John Montgomery, BioCryst Pharmaceuticals

Pages 109–111 Luis A. Barcena, Aechelon Technology Inc.

Page 112 Mark Peercy/SGI. Three-dimensional model courtesy of Milai Corporation, Japan

Page 114 *A Delineation of the Strata of England and Wales with Part of Scotland,* by William Smith (1815). The British Library

Page 117 Diagrams from Bela Julescz, *Foundations of Cyclopean Perception,* University of Chicago Press, Chicago, 1971, p. 95. ©1971 by Bell Telephone Laboratories, Inc. All rights reserved.

Page 122 "After the Storm: Considerations for Information Visualization" by Pauline Baker and Colleen Bushell, NCSA-TRO29, January 1995, Figure 4

Pages 124 and 127 Anne Treisman, *Scientific American* (1986) Volume 255, No. 5, pp. 116 & 120

Page 126 U.S. Geological Survey

Page 128 Image based on J. T. Enns & R.A. Rensink, "Influence of Scene-Based Properties on Visual Search," *Science,* (1990) Volume 247, p. 721

Page 130 *Haystacks, End of Summer* by Claude Monet (1840–1926)/Musée d'Orsay, Paris, France. Photograph by Erich Lessing/Art Resource

INDEX

Selected Books in the Scientific American Library Series

If you would like to purchase additional volumes in the
Scientific American Library, please send your order to:

Scientific American Library
41 Madison Avenue
New York, NY   10010